I love beauty, purity and authenticity,
because that is what moves people. Granted,
it takes courage to live life authentically,
but I believe it is the only way.

buy fresh

cook your
own meals

eat together

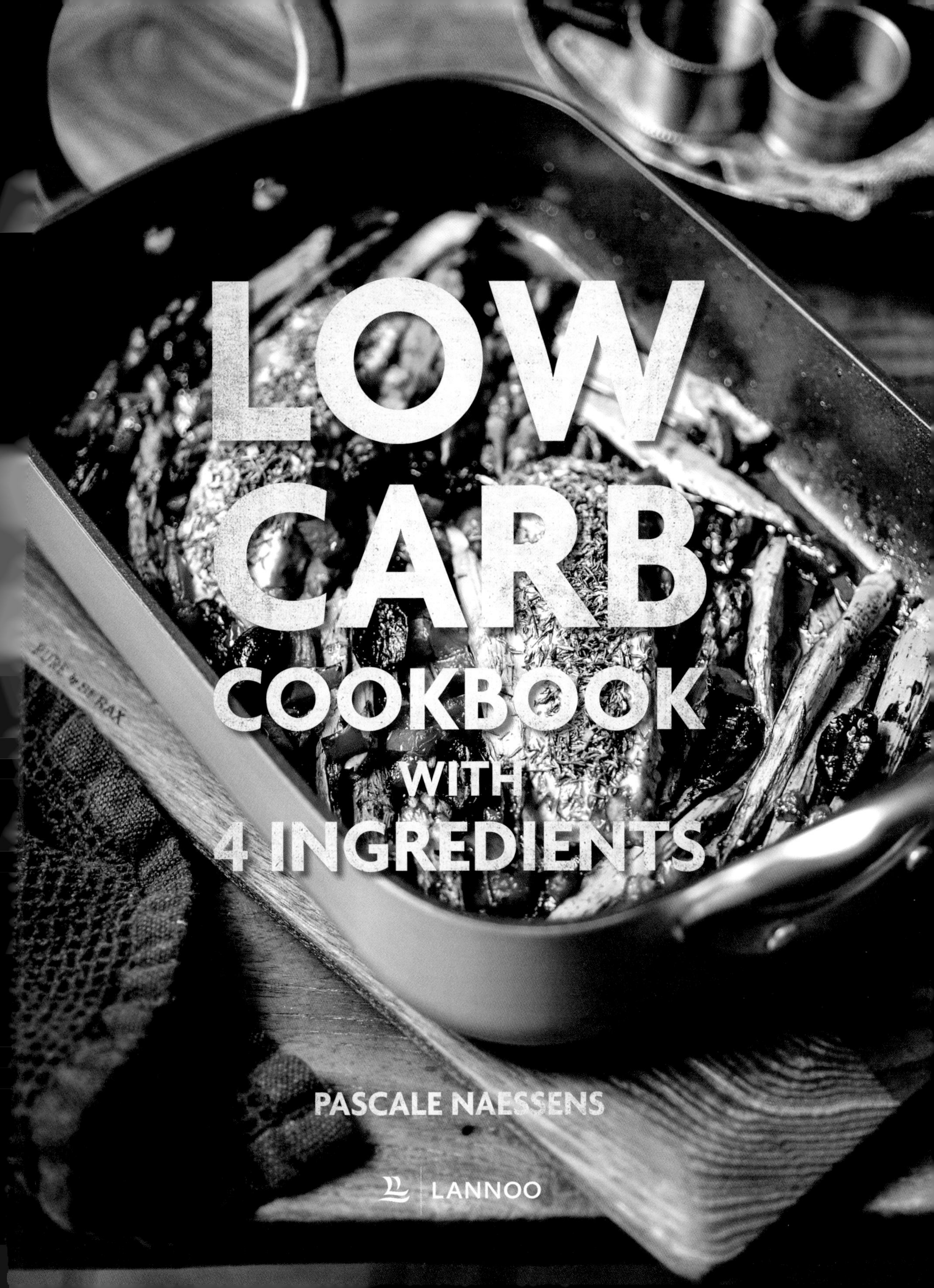

LOW
CARB
COOKBOOK
WITH
4 INGREDIENTS

PASCALE NAESSENS

LANNOO

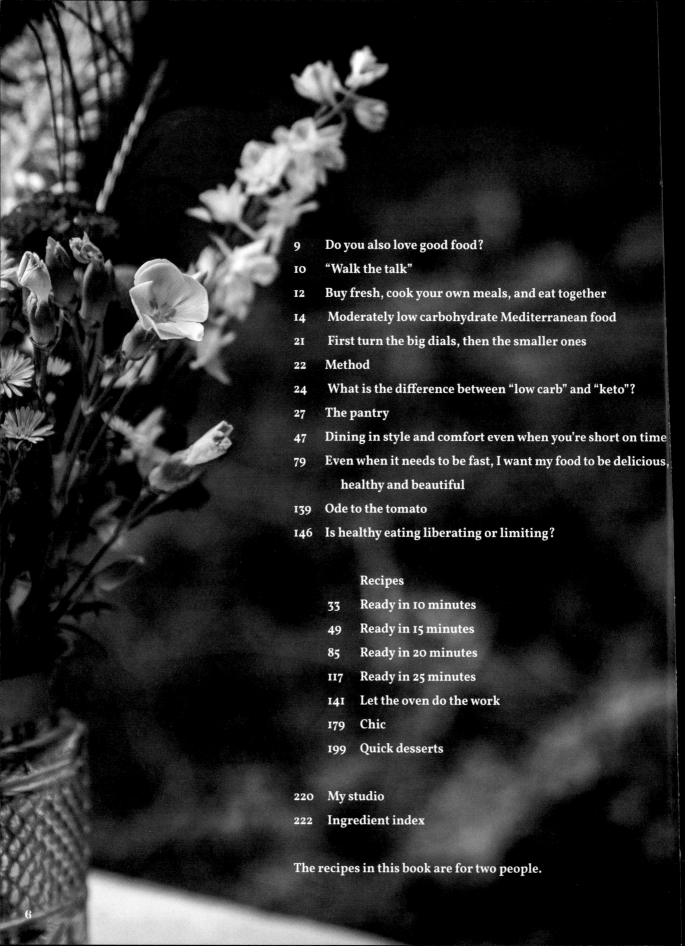

The recipes in this book are for two people.

Do you also love good food?

Handmade happiness

If you have bought or received this book that means that you're probably interested in healthy and delicious food just like I am. And you might already have an idea of how addictive eating "fresh" can be. I can't live without it these days. Even when it needs to be fast, I want my food to be delicious and healthy. I have written this book, where you will find recipes that take as little as 10 minutes to prepare. It's food that will make you happy in every respect. The recipes involve as little work as possible, so you will have the time to relax and enjoy them. Especially once you realize that these recipes will give you the energy you need, and that you can eat as much as you want without having to worry about the extra calories. I also want to mention the gorgeous colors. Because I use plenty of vegetables and herbs, each recipe simply radiates beauty and freshness. The fabulous colors and delicious smells instantly bring smiles to everyone's faces.
I call this handmade happiness.

This may be the book where I have had the most fun thinking up, testing, and making the recipes. Two years ago, I met a chef from New Zealand who always cooks with only four ingredients. I realized that this is something I had been doing myself for years without even thinking about it. I went and took a look at my very first book and saw that more than half my recipes consisted of four or even fewer ingredients. This has always been how I cook: making special recipes from just a few pure and basic ingredients.
Cookbooks with just four or five ingredients are not new, but for me it feels like coming home and going back to basics; cooking with as little effort as possible but with maximum results so you can enjoy your meal at the dinner table to the fullest. I also love to dine in style. When you surround yourself with beautiful and fun materials, you don't need much to make an everyday occurrence a moment of pure indulgence. No matter how little time I have, I want my moment at the dinner table to be one of rest and enjoyment.

I have poured my culinary heart and soul into this book, and now I would like to share it with you. I hope that it will inspire you, and that you will have as much fun using this book as I have had writing it.

Love,
Pascale

"Walk the talk"

My wife Stacey and I had the pleasure of being invited by Pascale and Paul for dinner at their house, a charming home with a living room featuring what was clearly the heart of the home; a gorgeous and prominent dining table. It soon became apparent that Pascale not only expresses her passion in speech, words and photos, but that she does this in her daily life as well. Or as the Americans aptly say, she "walks the talk". We had a delicious dinner at Pascale and Paul's, accompanied by animated conversation and a few glasses of wine while our hostess effortlessly conjured up one dish after the other at the dinner table. This is exactly as Pascale intended it to be. Because according to her, food is an experience, and since that evening I now know exactly how that feels and tastes.

Pascale is a one-of-a-kind phenomenon in the Dutch-speaking world. Not only does she produce the most amazing dishes but she also does so in a unique way, which appeals to me whichever way I look at it. Pascale has, through years of personal study and a constant dialogue with important researchers from all over the world, developed into what I would call an expert on healthy daily nutrition. Furthermore, she combines this with recipes that not only stand out for their flavors and presentation but also for their simplicity. It's also important to be able to produce quick and easy dishes because we live in a hectic world and we already have so much to do. When we cook for others, we also want to be enjoying each other's company instead of standing in the kitchen all evening. The recipes in this book make it all possible. Pascale has once again raised the bar to new heights. So simple!

William Cortvriendt

William Cortvriendt is a medical doctor and author of various bestsellers about nutrition and health, among which *Living a Century or More - A Scientifically Fact-Based Journey to Longevity*.

Buy fresh, cook your own meals, and eat together

Buy fresh

Healthy and flavorful food starts with high-quality, fresh, full-fat products. This is, by far, the best nutrition. I can't begin to count the number of times people tell me: "I eat so much better than I used to. My food has become tasty again, and I always leave the table full and satisfied." Have we really lost our way so badly that we believe that pre-fab meals and products even come close to natural sources of nutrition? Maybe we should have a little more faith in our own nature. Healthier eating has little to do with willpower. As a matter of fact, it has nothing to do with power at all. Instead of fighting your body, you should be working together with it. And you can do that by eating the food that your body is made to eat: natural and fresh food. You will be surprised how strongly your body reacts to this type of food. I have seen many people flourish: people who no longer want to go back to the addictive mass-produced, pre-fabricated foods which leave you feeling flab and drab and crush all your natural appetites. Would you like a powerful body full of energy? Then there is only one option. Buy high-quality, full, fresh, unprocessed and natural food.

High-quality: untreated fruits and vegetables, meat from animals that have had a good life.
Whole: nutrition which still contains all its natural fats and nutrients, for example full-fat yogurt instead of low-fat, real butter instead of margarine and certainly no light products. These foods are also known as "whole foods".
Fresh: fresh is actually really easy to recognize simply because fresh food tends to rot after a while. That's normal, that's how it should be. It's living food that contributes to the bacteria in our intestines. Think of vegetables, fruit, fish, meat, natural butter, eggs, full-fat yogurt…
Unprocessed: Food which has been processed as little as possible, which still has all its original fats and nutrients and has no additional flavors or additives. We just want simple, pure, natural products, and that means no light products, no margarines, no processed breakfast cereal or artificial products…

Discover or rediscover the charms of the market, where primarily fresh food is sold. If you cook with fresh products, you will have to spend a little more time doing the shopping, but that doesn't have to be a burden. Turn it into a fun outing. Deep down inside, we all know that fresh food forms the basis for a properly functioning body, and that in turn forms the basis for feeling healthy and happy. Consider your shopping trip as a form of indulgence.

Cook your own meals

Cooking your own food can be fast and it is fun to do, not to mention deeply satisfying. Moreover, cooking for yourself and others is a labor of love. A home with a well-used kitchen is a warm home, both literally and figuratively. This doesn't mean that you have to spend hours slaving away in the kitchen; on the contrary! The fun lies in being creative. I love the challenge of using just a few, pure ingredients and as little effort as possible to create an amazing meal. This is what makes cooking really fun. Of course, I also love to go out for dinner and if I am really strapped for time, I buy a healthy ready-made salad. But, as far as I am concerned, nothing beats having a delicious and convivial meal at home.

Eat together

The dining table is the perfect place to learn the art of conversation, especially in today's world of social media. Eating together is much more than just fueling your body. It is about connecting and sharing with each other. These are the real pleasures in life: sharing a nourishing, homemade meal together in a relaxed and convivial setting. This is why I do what I do, to experience these unique moments together with my loved ones. You can create these moments yourself too. It is in your hands.

This is the best guarantee for a long and healthy life. It works better than any medicine.

Moderately low carbohydrate Mediterranean food

is the best description of this way of eating.

Why Mediterranean food?

Because of the abundance of Mediterranean fruits and vegetables, and the widespread use of olive oil and plenty of fish.

Why moderately low carbohydrate?

Because certain carbohydrate-rich foods are limited, especially the fast-burning carbohydrates such as bread, potatoes, white rice, pasta, sugar, sweetened soft drinks …

Moderate because fiber-rich and naturally carbohydrate-rich foods are allowed: fruit, carbohydrate-rich vegetables (carrots, peas …), quinoa, oatmeal, lentils …
Compared to what we call "low carb" around the world (see further on), we can call it "moderate".

Why would you want to eat moderately low carbohydrate Mediterranean food?
>   Because:
>   - it is one of the world's most delicious cuisines;
>   - it makes you healthier with every bite;
>   - it gives you more energy;
>   - it will slim you down if you are overweight;
>   - it can probably help cut down or control type 2 diabetes (1)(2);
>   - it lowers the chance of cardiovascular disease (3);
>   - it lowers your blood pressure;
>   - it makes your gut happy;
>   - it makes you happy.

(1) Dietary carbohydrate restriction as the first approach in diabetes management: Critical review and evidence base
(2) Keer diabetes2 om. https://keerdiabetesom.nl/
(3) https://www.hsph.harvard.edu/nutritionsource/carbohydrates/low-carbohydrate-diets/

A further explanation of the term 'low carb'.

The term "low carb" is meaningless unless you can compare it to something else.
"Fewer carbohydrates", fewer than what? If you want to understand this term properly,
you need to link it to how we eat today in the Western world.

Our nutrition has evolved in a very short time from a natural cuisine to fast food, which for the
most part consists of refined carbohydrates (carbs). Think of processed grains: white bread,
cookies, cakes, packaged sauces, thickeners, pasta, white rice, sugar, soft drinks, etc.

We eat this "fake food" in addition to the potato, which in many cases still forms the basis of every
well-stocked kitchen. In the West, we have developed a carbohydrate-rich diet in a relatively short
period of time. Besides the potato, we have a whole arsenal of processed carbs that have become
the daily staples of our basic diet.

The term "high carb" is apt when we talk about our Western diet. The question then remains,
which term do we adopt for the diet of someone who cooks with primarily fresh products,
who avoids refined carbohydrates, and who keeps potatoes to a minimum? I believe we can
call this type of eating pattern "normal carb".

Now that you have a better understanding of these terms, let's talk about "low carb". Everyone
agrees that we need to cut down on fast carbs such as white bread, white rice, soft drinks and
such. There's no doubt about that. The discussion starts when we need to decide how high to raise
the bar with regards to the amount of carbs we should be eating. Well, that differs from person
to person. That's why we should stop arguing and start listening to each other and—especially—
to our own bodies instead. The only interesting question that still remains is why someone would
choose to eat fewer carbs. People often have good reasons for doing so.

One important thing to note in the entire discussion around diets in general, and 'low carb' in
particular, is that most people assume that everyone should be eating in the same way. But look
around you… we are all different and nobody has the same body shape. While one person can
eat plenty and stay at their ideal weight, another may gain weight eating the same amount.
Why should we all have to eat the same things? We all react differently to food. That's also true for
carbohydrate-rich food: some people can eat plenty of carbs without gaining weight, while other
people immediately gain weight and become addicted to boot. I belong to that second group.

I am one of those people who reacts strongly to (fast) carbs, who immediately gains weight and becomes addicted to them as well.

That's why I have removed practically all (fast) carbs from my diet and have limited my intake of fiber-rich whole carbs such as lentils, quinoa, beans and chickpeas. If the proportion of carbs in my diet becomes too great, even of the healthier carbohydrates, then it feels as if I'm losing control of my body. I feel an insatiable hunger and lose control over my appetite. My whole body feels out of sync and I feel miserable. I get extreme hunger pangs and cravings, which leaves me constantly thinking about food in an unhealthy, obsessive way. Then I end up feeling bad and I start having doubts and depressing thoughts. When I eat fewer carbs and more fatty products —such as nuts, full-fat yogurt and olive oil—and I gorge on vegetables, the process reverses itself and I retain that naturally full and satisfied feeling. I feel happy with my body and I can feel my energy levels rise. Moreover, I love this way of eating because it feels so natural. I think it's a shame that people who eat "differently" should constantly have to defend themselves. Why should they? Because it makes them feel better?

How low you should go with your carb intake depends on how your body reacts and what you want to achieve. Most people benefit from the moderate carbohydrate diet that you'll find in my books. They experience many health benefits: more energy, better blood values, fewer aches and pains as the excess pounds disappear, a return to a more balanced appetite and a reduction in type 2 diabetes. No less than 87% of diabetes patients can completely or partly reverse their type 2 diabetes with the help of a low-carb diet.

Some people need to go one step further and lower their carb intake even more in order to reap the benefits. For example, people with resistance to insulin or stubborn weight issues, or patients who have been suffering from severe chronic type 2 diabetes. They tell me that they must keep a close eye on their carbohydrate intake and that it's best for them to avoid even the healthy, fiber-rich carbohydrates such as oatmeal, certain fruits and beans.

The ketogenic diet (or keto diet, for short) takes it a step further. With this diet you limit your carbohydrate intake to less than 2 ounces (50 grams) per day, combined with a normal quantity of protein and plenty of fats. With this diet, your blood sugar level remains at a constantly low level and your body almost exclusively starts burning fat. Your liver starts producing ketones to feed your brain. That's where the name "ketogenic diet" comes from.

Some opponents claim that this type of diet is unhealthy, possibly because it deviates too much from the traditional and generally accepted norms. However, recent scientific studies have shown mostly positive benefits: weight loss, beneficial effects for people with epilepsy, and even promising results with cancer treatments.

Just to clarify: you should not be leaving carbohydrates out altogether, even with a keto diet. That's practically impossible anyway, because many foods contain carbohydrates, including vegetables. A keto diet is fairly radical and socially not easy to manage, but it's certainly not impossible. Would you like to follow a keto diet? Seek guidance from a professional, especially if you have diabetes. For more information about the keto diet, see page 24.

Conclusion

How many or how few carbs you should eat varies for each individual. You need to listen to your own body to figure out what works for you. What do you want to achieve? What feels right to you? Read about it and experiment. Experience for yourself the difference between more and fewer carbs, so you know what effect carbs have on your body. That's the only way to gain insight into the conflicting messages we receive about low-carb foods and nutrition.

I would like to add that eating moderately low carb is absolutely delicious, far tastier than the one-sided, traditional, Western, carbohydrate-rich diet, and that it's very easy to maintain. Anyone saying the contrary either hasn't tried it yet or is strongly addicted to carbs. They can't stay away from the (fast) carbs—not because the high-carb foods are so delicious, but because they are addictive. I know that feeling all too well, because I've been there. As soon as you are released from your addiction, you'll feel liberated and discover a delicious cuisine that will truly make you happy. Just have a look through this book if I haven't convinced you yet.

Important note:
Some people can eat plenty of fast carbs without gaining weight. Sometimes people come up to me and tell me with pride how they can eat plenty of chips, potatoes, bread and even chocolate bars and still stay slim. But being slim on the outside doesn't necessarily mean that you're healthy on the inside. You may have already heard of TOFI: **thin outside, fat inside.**

Doctor William Cortvriendt sums it up as follows: "Slim people who eat lots of fast carbs have in their blood all the factors which can lead to problems with joints, diabetes, or cardiovascular disease later in life, just like people who are overweight."

Do you want to live a good life? Stay close to what feels natural to you and eat high-quality, fresh food.

Hidden sugars

Bread, white rice, pasta, potatoes … they all contain plenty of starch, which is basically just one long sugar molecule. As Professor Mozaffarian says: "Starch is a hidden sugar. If you don't think about how rapidly starch and sugar in the foods that you are eating are digested, you are going to make incorrect eating decisions. The dose and rapid digestion of starches and sugars in our foods—this is one of the things driving the obesity and diabetes epidemic."
http://now.tufts.edu/articles/carb-ranking-controversy

Fewer carbohydrates but more fats

If you leave something out of your eating pattern, in this case (fast) carbs, you need to replace it with something else. And that will only work if that something else is tastier, better and healthier: vegetables, fruit and—oh yes—FAT! More fat doesn't only mean tastier, because fat adds flavor, but it gives richness to meals so that you regain that natural satisfied feeling. It is, however, important not to eat more proteins (meat or fish) but to eat more vegetables and fat.

Eating more fat, how do you do that?

We're talking about fat from natural, whole foods:

- If you use olive oil, don't use it sparingly, but pour it all in there. It makes your food tastier, more attractive and healthier.

- Stop counting calories, and use fresh and natural whole foods, such as fatty fish, nuts, full-fat yogurt, avocado, olive oil, seeds … all ingredients that have a positive effect on our health, even though they may be rich in calories.

- Don't use light products such as margarines and low-fat yogurt.

People who want to stay slim or lose weight shouldn't eat less, but should eat higher quality food:

- mostly fresh, natural ingredients;

- more full-fat natural ingredients;

- less sugar and starch.

What if that's how I eat, and I still don't lose any weight?

- Then you're at the weight that matches your body type.

- Do you have doubts and want to be sure? Visit your primary care physician for a check-up. If you're healthy, keep eating the way you are and read the following points carefully.

- Your body needs time to adjust.

- Losing weight is not a straightforward process. Most people lose more weight in the first week, but that's mostly water; after the first week, the process is slower. Losing weight often happens in stages. You'll level out for a while and then suddenly you'll lose a few pounds again. It is important that you feel healthy and keep eating varied, fresh foods. Enjoy the delicious food and try not to worry about the weight. Think long-term.

- Some people are more sensitive to carbs than others. In that case, you will have to cut back on your carb intake even more. Perhaps you're eating too many healthy sugars such as bananas, grapes or honey? Banana bread with oatmeal is not a good choice if you want to lose weight.

- You're stressed the whole time and don't sleep well. It is generally known that stress raises the levels of the cortisol hormone, which stimulates your appetite. Go for a walk, exercise or do something creative. If you have trouble managing your stress, look for professional help.

- You eat too little fresh food and too much "healthy" pre-packaged food, such as oatmeal bars, breakfast cereals, salads with honey dressing and sweetened cranberries …
These (often) contain hidden sugars, refined starches and processed fats. Cook fresh and don't be too stingy with the fat. Make sure that you get that full feeling—the right way.

- You snack too much. Try to stick to three meals a day and eat only when you're "really" hungry. Snacking is a habit and usually has little to do with being hungry. Some people think that they can eat nuts all day and therefore eat plenty of nuts between meals, even when they're not feeling hungry. But too much of anything is never a good thing.

- You resort too often to comfort food. While comfort food may not be a problem for some, for others, especially people with an addictive nature, it can be problem. In that case, the occasional comfort food binge does more harm than good. I am a prime example of that. If you cannot control yourself when you're confronted with unhealthy food, then you might be addicted to it. In that case, the only option is to ban processed food completely from your life.

-   You have unrealistic expectations. We're not all built for a size 8. Some people are tall and slim, while others are petite and stocky. Everyone has a "set point": this is a natural balance where you can eat as much healthy food as you want without having to think twice about it and without gaining or losing weight. And if you want to get below that balance, you will have to diet. That means eating less food than your body needs, which is almost impossible to maintain. The other way around is just as big a problem. People who are underweight have a hard time gaining weight and will always have to eat more. But, as soon as they stop, their body will return to their original weight, the "set point". In that case, power training and developing muscle tissue might be the solution.

-   The most important question you need to ask yourself is: how do I feel? As I wrote earlier, we don't all have to be a size 8. Be yourself, be pure and be happy. That's what counts.

"The research lends strong support to the notion that diet quality, not quantity, is what helps people lose and manage their weight most easily in the long run. It also suggests that health authorities should shift away from telling the public to obsess over calories and instead encourage people to avoid processed foods that are made with refined starches and added sugar, like bagels, white bread, refined flour and sugary snacks and beverages" said Dr. Dariush Mozaffarian, cardiologist and dean of the Friedman School of Nutrition Science and Policy at Tufts University in Boston.

Effect of Low-Fat vs Low-Carbohydrate Diet on 12-Month Weight Loss in Overweight Adults and the Association With Genotype Pattern or Insulin Secretion: The DIETFITS Randomized Clinical Trial.
JAMA. 2018;319(7):667-679. doi:10.1001/jama.2018.0245

More information about low-carbohydrate foods

In my other cookbooks, I have written to a greater extent about the science behind the low-carb movement as well as plenty of 'moderately low carb' recipes.

First turn the big dials, then the smaller ones

Many people don't know where to start. People sometimes ask me questions such as: "Which nuts are the healthiest?" But … it doesn't help to think about these details when you're eating the wrong things in the first place. So first turn the big dials: eat fresh, unprocessed food and limit your intake of sugars and starchy foods. Try turning it into your new way of life, because that will bring about the biggest change in your life and your health. As soon as you have that down, you can continue to build on that and tweak the smaller dials, such as finding out which fruits, vegetables and nuts work best for you. It's a fascinating and enlightening journey, but it's also important to do it one step at a time. Just start where you are now and build it up slowly.

Losing weight

People who are overweight will, with the help of these recipes, find a natural way to lose weight permanently. By "natural", I mean without too much willpower, but simply by respecting the rules of the game where our bodies are concerned. People eating fresh, high-quality ingredients will automatically eat moderately low carb. Our bodies react surprisingly positively to this. This moderately low-carb Mediterranean eating pattern is one of the easiest, and at the same time most valuable keys to a healthier and slimmer life. (Read more on page 14.)

Gaining weight

Besides people who want to lose weight, there are also people who want to gain weight, although I have to admit that these people are definitely in the minority. But, I do frequently get the question: "How can I gain weight in a healthy way?" Well, that's not so simple. We all have our own "set point", what we call our natural weight when we eat healthily. If you want to go below this point, you will have to diet every day, I mean really diet. This means eating less food than your body needs, which is difficult to maintain. But the other way around is an equally big problem. If you want to gain weight above your "set point", you will always have to eat "more", and as soon as you stop eating extra, your body will return to its original weight, to the "set point". If you are underweight, have yourself examined by a doctor. If you are healthy, then keep on eating healthy foods and definitely don't start eating unhealthy refined foods simply to gain weight. What often does work is power training. This increases your muscle tissue and more muscle is healthier. Don't feel intimidated by the term "power training". You may just need to give it a chance because it can be quite fun.

Method

Putting the theory into practice is not always easy. That's why I have adopted a method with only one rule. People who stick to this rule will make better choices in their daily lives. It will ensure that you will automatically start eating moderately "low carb".

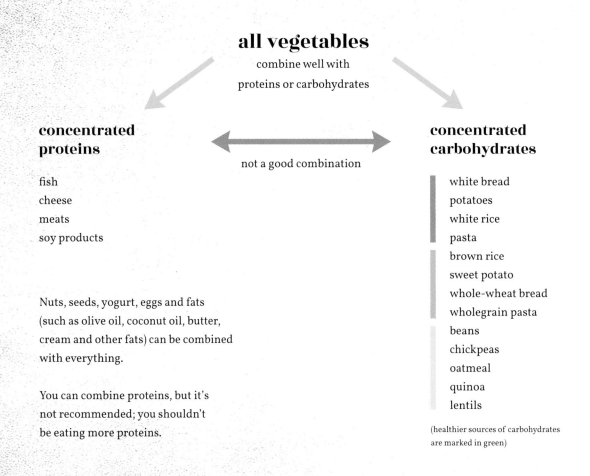

all vegetables
combine well with
proteins or carbohydrates

not a good combination

concentrated proteins

fish
cheese
meats
soy products

Nuts, seeds, yogurt, eggs and fats
(such as olive oil, coconut oil, butter,
cream and other fats) can be combined
with everything.

You can combine proteins, but it's
not recommended; you shouldn't
be eating more proteins.

concentrated carbohydrates

white bread
potatoes
white rice
pasta
brown rice
sweet potato
whole-wheat bread
wholegrain pasta
beans
chickpeas
oatmeal
quinoa
lentils

(healthier sources of carbohydrates
are marked in green)

It is better not to eat protein-rich foods together with carbohydrate-rich foods. In practice, this means that you will often replace potatoes and bread with fruits, vegetables and fats. This will encourage you to eat more fresh food and make your eating habits simpler and clearer. You will find this principle of making the right combinations in many cultures and it's certainly not new. All I have done is converted this information into a handy diagram that is practical for use in daily life. This is a practical application of all the latest and most relevant scientific discoveries: more fresh food, fewer (fast) carbohydrates, more fats and moderate protein intake. Every healthy eating pattern is about maintaining balance. When you are out of balance (because you're eating too much processed food and too little fresh food, for instance), problems arise. This method keeps you in balance. You can find more information about healthy food combinations in any of my other books and on my website: www.purepascale.com

I hate diets and I don't like the word "health" either. But I do love my slim, energetic body.

I love this life, I love being full of energy and I love good food. That's why I live and eat as I do now —completely according to my wild nature. I enjoy life to the fullest and sometimes I make mistakes with my voracious lust for life. It's part of who I am and what keeps life interesting. But, I don't eat and live to be healthy! The word health has been "hijacked" and has very little to do with enjoyment anymore. Today, we think about health in terms of black and white: the healthy people versus the unhealthy people. This word is being used to judge and label people and that's an unfortunate development because it divides people in a meaningless way. It's essentially about being happy: feeling good in your body, living with full awareness, getting the most out of life. Savoring life! I feel that this is something everyone deserves.

What is the difference between "low carb" and "keto"?

Keto belongs to the family of diets that includes paleo, Atkins, and low carb. **You can categorize all these diets under the "low carb" header, the way of eating which I have been working on for years. The only nuanced differences are the relative proportions of carbohydrates, fats and proteins.** My way of eating follows the same principles, but I have deliberately avoided using these names in the past because they tend to lead to a lot of criticism. Some may see them as extreme, but that is more due to lack of knowledge. However, the low carb diet movement has become unstoppable, because they encourage weight loss and because of the many health benefits that they offer. Today, many doctors and specialists have introduced these diets into their practice. We are clearly a step further than ten years ago when I started writing cookbooks. And I can say with pride that I have been able to help lead that change. Low carb, which includes almost all the recipes from this book and from my earlier books, is becoming increasingly mainstream. I also notice this from the many positive reactions that I receive from my books, and also from the many requests that I receive from specialists asking me to work with them. Consider the low carb movement as one big family, containing many differences and nuances. Keto is one of those.

Keto is a very strict version of low carb. In a keto diet, you also avoid the so-called "healthy carbohydrates", such as oatmeal, lentils, beans, and other carbohydrate-rich vegetables such as peas, parsnips and sweet potatoes as well as some carbohydrate-rich fruits. The idea is that you eat as few carbs as possible (only 1 to 2 ounces (20-50 grams) carbs per day), forcing your body to switch from burning sugars to burning fats. This is a huge benefit for people who are overweight, because their fat reserves finally get used up, causing them to lose weight in a spectacular and permanent fashion without them having to starve themselves. Losing weight is, therefore, the most common reason to "go keto". The advantages are the same as low carb, but with keto, they're more extreme.

Your body prefers sugar as a source of energy because sugars are the easiest to convert. Without sugar, your liver will produce more ketones as a source of energy, hence the name "keto diet". This diet is not new because before the agricultural revolution, people had little access to carbs, or at least certainly not every day. The body of the hunter-gatherer was often in a ketogenic state. Newborn babies also use fat as an initial source of energy and produce ketones. Or if someone is fasting, by choice or by force, the body also produces more ketones. It is a natural metabolic state in the body.

You can eat moderately low carb, meaning that you can also eat fruit, lentils and quinoa, but you cannot eat moderately keto. Ketosis is a metabolic state and either your body is in it or it is not. Someone who happens to eat something rich in sugars will immediately go out of the keto state.

Moreover, it is not easy to reach ketosis. Many people think that they eat keto because they eat few carbohydrates, but it's not as simple as that. It is also dependent on the amount of fats and protein you eat and the way your body reacts to this. The only trustworthy way to know whether you're in ketosis is to measure the ketone values in your blood. This can be done using a meter, with which you measure your ketones the same way that you would test your glucose, by taking a blood sample. This, however, is quite expensive.

The proportions of an average keto diet on any given day are: 80% fat, 10% carbohydrates and 25% protein. (Jeff Volek and Stephen Phinney, *The Art and Science of Low Carbohydrate Living*)

Conclusion:

Keto is a powerful way to lose weight and to gain a healthier body. But it requires knowledge. You need to know what you're doing, because it requires a very strict eating regimen and because you need to be consistent. Therefore, it's socially not easy to manage, but it's certainly not impossible. I know people who have been in ketosis for years, who feel absolutely fine and see this as their new way of life. They use almost all my recipes, except the ones featuring lentils, chickpeas, oatmeal and sugary fruits such as bananas. **All keto-friendly recipes in this book are indicated by this symbol** ✓ keto. An excellent site where you can find many practical tips, and video interviews with professionals, is www.dietdoctor.com. The founder of this site about low carb and keto is Dr. Andreas Eenfeldt, with whom I work and to whom I provide recipes.

Important note

Many people think they eat keto, but they're actually eating low carb. There is nothing wrong with that, on the contrary. Low carb is enough for most people to gain all the positive benefits, such as weight loss, more energy, better blood values, no more sweet cravings, and most type 2 diabetes patients can even turn their type 2 diabetes around. The advantage of low carb is that it is more moderate and therefore easier to maintain. Your goals are dependent on your own body and what you personally would like to achieve. We need to dare to think further than the simplistic vision that everyone can and should follow the same "perfect diet"' during every stage of their lives.

Nutritional ketosis and ketoacidosis

Nutritional ketosis is a natural metabolic state that, over the course of history, has given people the flexibility to deal with both changes in the food supply and times of hunger. Ketoacidosis, however, is an unstable and dangerous condition that develops when the pancreas is only partially, or no longer, able to produce the insulin required to manage the ketone levels in the body. This only occurs in type 1 diabetes and patients with a severe and chronic type 2 diabetes condition. Unfortunately, these two metabolic states sometimes get mixed up. Being aware of this is, therefore, crucial. I recommend that all diabetic patients who are considering embarking on a keto diet seek out the guidance of a professional.

the pantry

The guiding principle in this book is that you only need to buy 4 ingredients for any one dish. These are usually fresh ingredients. The rest I consider to be basic ingredients, which you will always have at home. These are not listed in the ingredients list but are found in the pantry (marked with the icon above). For people who want to make the most of this book, I recommend that you get the basic ingredients first. You might even have most of these at home already.

Considering that we don't use many ingredients, it is important that all the ingredients are of the highest quality, because one bad ingredient can ruin your meal. Hunting down the finest quality requires some detective work and research, but it is a fun and educational exercise, which is certainly worth the effort.

These are the ingredients that you should always have in your pantry; they are not included in the 4-ingredients list.

Fats	Vinegar	Flavorings	Extra
olive oil	balsamic vinegar	soy sauce	coconut sugar
butter	apple cider vinegar	mustard	
coconut oil			

Herbs and Spices
black pepper
fleur de sel
ras-el-hanout
dried Herbes de Provence: thyme, rosemary…
garlic (dried or fresh)
cumin

One more practical tip:
Parchment paper is also handy to have around the house. I make many desserts or egg dishes in baking dishes lined with parchment paper. Once the dessert has cooled, I can simply lift it out of the dish. Moreover, you don't have to do any scrubbing afterwards because there is nothing to scrape off the dish.

Fats

Extra-virgin olive oil: this is my basic kitchen fat, exceptionally tasty and one of the healthiest fats around. Not all olive oils are the same. Choose an extra-virgin olive oil to get oil from the first cold pressing, before it has been processed in any way. If you want, you can buy more expensive oil for the cold dishes, because they often have a subtler flavor, and a cheaper oil to cook with; in that case, still choose extra-virgin olive oil because it's healthier, tastier, and unprocessed.

Butter: butter is delicious! Choose the real, natural stuff because it's much tastier and healthier than the fake butters that are out there. Butter can lift a boring dish up to new culinary heights, giving the dish extra flavor and fullness. Choose dairy butter made from the milk of grass-fed cows, living on their natural diet.

Coconut oil: just like with all the other fats, we choose the extra-virgin variety. This is the least processed oil, obtained from the first cold press. It is a deliciously creamy fat, which can lend an Asian touch to your dishes. It is also ideal for frying at higher temperatures.

Vinegar

Balsamic vinegar: vinegar made from reduced grape juice that has been aged in wooden barrels. Here, too, you will find significant differences in taste and quality. You don't have to buy the most expensive variety, but certainly don't go for the cheapest one either as these are often sour-tasting and watery. If the vinegar tastes sweet, caramel or sugar has been added to it. A high-quality *aceto balsamico* has been aged in wooden barrels for several years and does not contain any preservatives or other ingredients. It is the number of years that the vinegar has aged that dictates the price and quality of the vinegar. Only after 12 years can you speak of an *aceto balsamico tradizionale di Modena*, the key word here being "tradizionale" (traditional). Between the cheapest and most expensive varieties you can find many good-quality balsamic vinegars. Good balsamic vinegar is syrupy, smells delicious and has a full, subtle, sweet and sour taste.

Apple cider vinegar: delicious and subtle vinegar made from fermented apple juice. The cloudy version is, in principle, better than the clearer variety because the latter has been filtered several times, but the cloudy vinegar is harder to find. I often use this vinegar in the kitchen because it adds depth of flavor to a dish without that sharp, sour taste that most vinegars tend to have. Moreover, this fermented vinegar is also exceptionally healthy.

Flavorings

Soy sauce: this Asian fermented sauce made from soybeans has already secured a favored spot in the Western kitchen. Sometimes it can take a while to find the sauce that best suits your tastes because there is such a wide variety of sauces. I prefer the milder soy sauce, which is less salty and widely available in all supermarkets. But, when I get the chance, I like to step into an Asian specialty food store to hunt down a soy sauce with a longer fermentation period, packaged in a beautiful bottle. Not only does it look good on the table, it is also much subtler in taste.

Mustard: you can create so many surprising tastes with mustard. It is an ideal way to give more taste and texture to your sauce. Mustard is made from the mustard plant, a beautiful plant with yellow flowers, from which pods grow carrying the mustard seeds. These seeds are mixed with the basic ingredients: water, salt, and vinegar. Each manufacturer uses their own seed blend and adds other ingredients such as turmeric or even oil. I prefer mild mustard. High-quality mustard is, of course, a natural product without any added sugars.

Sugar: I only use sugar in my desserts. Ideally, I like to use coconut sugar because I love its caramel taste, and honey. Both are unrefined sugars. Don't get me wrong; it doesn't make it any healthier because sugar is, after all, still sugar. Even low-calorie sweeteners have negative effects. All sugars, whether they're rich or low in calories, maintain and stimulate the craving for sweetness, especially when combined with the ingredients with which you tend to use them. So when you add sweeteners—and it doesn't matter which one—you will always run the risk of eating more than you need. People who want to lose weight or who have an addictive sweet tooth should probably stay away from the desserts. Sometimes it is easier to avoid the sweet stuff altogether than to occasionally eat something sweet. Don't forget that, when you eat according to this book, your sugar cravings will also lessen. Honest! I rarely prepare desserts at home, except on special occasions. And, even then, I use as little sugar as possible, or even no sugar at all, as I do with the *Chocolate with peanut butter* recipe on page 215. So don't worry, you'll still be eating well, and you won't have to deny yourself anything.

Herbs and Spices

Ras-el-hanout: most herbs and spices don't need an introduction, but I do want to take a moment to talk about ras-el-hanout. This is a North African spice blend and its name can be loosely translated as "top of the shop", or the best the store has to offer. Each store in North Africa has its own blend, but you can easily find it here now as well. The most important spices are cinnamon, ginger, coriander, chili pepper, nutmeg, turmeric, cloves… all of my favorite spices! With a jar of this stuff in your kitchen, you instantly have all the spices you need at home, ideal for when you need to be quick. The aroma and color are so intense that I want to put it in almost every dish. Ras-el-hanout is delicious with chicken, fish and vegetable dishes—in other words, with everything that you will find in this book.

4 ingredients, how about a little more?

In this book, we work with four ingredients. But don't let this stop you from adding extra ingredients to the dishes, such as extra (fresh) herbs and vegetables. Get creative! Anything goes. Just don't forget that these basic recipes are also excellent in their own right.

"Tips and tricks" for people who cook with little time and few ingredients
People who work with just a few ingredients need to cook smart. I'll give you a few golden tips to take simple dishes to the next level:

Fresh herbs: grow your own herbs. Thyme and rosemary last through the winter and you can even grow them easily in pots. Incorporate fresh herbs into your dishes or sprinkle some freshly chopped herbs over your dish just before serving; they make all the difference and instantly turn you into a gourmet cook.

Gomashio: I use this to garnish my stews and stir-fries. It is not always easy to present these dishes in an appealing manner. My tip is: use a deep dish and garnish your dish with some gomashio. It adds sparkle to even the simplest of dishes. Gomashio is used in Japanese cuisine and is made from ground, roasted sesame seeds with a little salt. Again, choose quality, because the cheaper versions have flavorings or even sugar added to them.

Nuts and seeds: I often add nuts and seeds to my meals, especially dishes with lots of vegetables and cheese. It adds color (especially pistachios), flavor and texture. I also often use sesame seeds as a garnish. This transforms a simple dish into a beautiful and creative whole. Moreover, it gives the dish a crunchy texture.

Lime and lemon: there are always a couple of limes or lemons lying in my fruit bowl. A little drizzle of this naturally sour flavor instantly adds depth of flavor to a dish.

Curry paste: it is always useful to have red and green curry paste around the house. It works like magic; one teaspoon is often enough to transform a simple dish into an explosion of tastes. It also keeps for a long time, even after the jar has been opened. Always keep the opened jar of curry paste in the fridge.

Fresh ginger and turmeric: I always have these in my kitchen. Add them to stir-fried vegetables for an immediate wow-effect. Moreover, these roots keep for a long time. I place them in a bowl next to the fruit bowl, adding atmosphere to the kitchen. Much has already been written about the medicinal benefits of these roots and nobody will deny their healing properties. They are a perfect fit in a delicious and healthy kitchen.

Garlic: I find fresh garlic an essential ingredient in the kitchen. I thought long and hard about whether to put it on the pantry list, but, ultimately, I decided not to do it. The reason is that fresh garlic keeps perhaps the least well of all the ingredients in the above list. And the pantry contains primarily ingredients that will keep for a long time. But if you want to cook with flair, I recommend that you always have fresh garlic around.

Star anise

Cinnamon

Cumin

Black pepper

Ras-el-hanout

Parsley

Rosemary

Fleur de sel

Coriander

Pink pepper

Turmeric

Thyme

ready in
10 minutes

The chapters in this book are divided according to the time you need to make a dish. The time starts from the moment that all the ingredients are out on your kitchen counter until the dish is ready to be served. It may be that you won't be able to prepare the dish in the given time the first time round, but chances are you'll succeed the second time round, and you may even have some time left over on the third try. Cooking is not a race against the clock, but it helps if you only need to spend 10 minutes getting a meal ready after a long day at work or during a short lunch break. Afterwards, you can take all the time you need to savor a delicious and healthy meal. This will give you peace and energy and make you happy.

Radicchio keto

with goat cheese and nuts

- **6 heads radicchio or endive**
- **2 fresh slices of goat cheese (or another favorite cheese)**
- **4 spring onions**
- **handful of pecans**

– balsamic vinegar –

Preheat the oven to 350 °F (180 °C). Cut the radicchio lengthwise in half and cook the
heads in a non-stick frying pan with the cut side down in some olive oil. Place the slices of
cheese in a baking dish and bake them for a few minutes in the oven until they start to melt.
Finely chop the spring onions.

After about 4 minutes, add a generous splash of balsamic vinegar to the radicchio and cook
for another 2 minutes. Divide the heads up over two plates.

Return the frying pan to the heat and add the pecan nuts and spring onions. If needed,
add a little olive oil and balsamic vinegar and cook them for a half or whole minute. Place the
melted cheese on the radicchio and scatter the roasted nuts and spring onions over the top.

TIP: GOAT CHEESE
I use ripe goat cheese and cut off the outer crust. You can, of course, use any cheese that you
like, as long as it melts slightly. Brie, for example, also works really well.

Red richness.

red vegetables
with lentils

- **7 oz (200 g) cooked lentils (see tip)**
- **4 tomatoes**
- **1 raw red beet (7 oz/200 g)**
- **2 tablespoons red curry paste**

Clean the red beet. You don't need to peel it. Slice the beet into thin slices. The easiest way to do this is to use a mandolin slicer. Cook the slices in plenty of olive oil, turning them over regularly.

Dice the tomatoes and remove the hard, white core. Cook them together with the red beet. Season with salt and pepper. Once the vegetables are tender, add the curry paste.

Add a spoonful of the paste at a time and taste as you go. Stir carefully until everything is warmed through. Meanwhile, warm the lentils in a splash of olive oil and season with salt and pepper. It goes even quicker when you just add the lentils to the vegetables, but I like to serve the lentils separately. Spoon the vegetables and lentils next to each other on a plate.

TIP: LENTILS AND BEANS, THE QUICK WAY
In the health food store, you can buy packages with pre-cooked pulse mixes or bean, lentil, quinoa or chickpea blends… These are very useful to have in the kitchen. Simply cook some fresh vegetables, add the pulse mix at the end and you have a delicious vegetarian dish in no time.

TIP: COOKING LENTILS YOURSELF
If you are cooking dried lentils, you will need approximately 3 ½ oz (100 g) lentils. They double in volume during the cooking process. I usually use green lentils, which are ready in 25 minutes.

For when you're not particularly hungry,
but still want to put something special on the table.

eggplant
with honey and sesame seeds

- **2 eggplants**
- **3 tablespoons honey**
- **roasted sesame seeds**

- 3 tablespoons soy sauce -

Slice the eggplant into ½-inch (1 cm) slices. Take a large frying pan and cook the eggplant in plenty of olive oil until cooked through. Remember, eggplant soaks up a lot of olive oil! Turn the slices over in time so they don't burn. Add an extra splash of olive oil if necessary.

Meanwhile, mix the soy sauce together with the honey and 1 tablespoon of olive oil. Add the sauce to the eggplant after 7 to 8 minutes of cooking. Remove the pan from heat, scatter the sesame seeds over the eggplant, turn the slices over and return the pan to the heat for another 30 seconds.

Serve the eggplant in a large dish or an attractive pan.

A fantastic dish: full of flavor, gorgeous colors and deliciously pink-cooked salmon.

pan-seared salmon

with vegetables

- **2 pieces of salmon, without the skin**
- **3 to 4 plum tomatoes**
- **handful of curly-leaf parsley**
- **3 garlic cloves**

Slice the garlic and finely chop the curly-leaf parsley. Slice the tomatoes.
Add a generous splash of olive oil to a large frying pan. Place the slices of garlic and the chopped parsley in the pan. Layer the tomato slices on top of the garlic. Place the pan on the heat for 3 minutes and then stir the vegetables.

Push the vegetables over to one side and add the salmon to the pan next to the vegetables.
Cook the salmon for a minute and a half on each side, leaving it still raw on the inside.
Place the salmon on a plate and spoon the vegetables over and next to the salmon.

lentils
with onions and bell peppers

- 10½ oz (300 g) cooked lentils
- 1 large onion (200 g/7 oz)
- 2 red bell peppers (see tip)
- 1½ oz (40 g) flat-leaf parsley

Slice the onion and bell pepper into thin rings and cook them for approximately 6 minutes in olive oil. Season with salt and pepper. Add the lentils and coarsely chopped parsley once the vegetables are cooked through.

TIP: RED BELL PEPPER
I often buy long, sweet, pointed bell peppers. These are easier to slice and have fewer seeds.

TIP: LEFTOVER RECIPE
I sometimes call this my leftover recipe as a joke. Do you have leftover vegetables lying about? Stir-fry them as well! It will just make your dish even tastier, and you get to clean out your fridge as well (also read p. 69).

*One of my favorite lunches,
wonderfully filling.*

This is my
personal favorite
ten-minute dish.

fish curry ✓keto

with spinach

- 10½ oz (300 g) white fish, such as wolffish or cod
- 10½ oz (300 g) spinach
- ½ to ¾ can of coconut milk (about 1 cup/200-300 ml)
- 3 to 4 tablespoons green curry paste

Pour the coconut milk into a pan and mix in the curry paste. Start with 2 to 3 tablespoons of curry paste. If you like your food spicy, you can always add in some extra curry paste at the end. Add a little water if the sauce is too thick. It should have the consistency of a thick soup.

Divide the fish into portions and place them in the sauce. Season with some salt and pepper. Place the spinach leaves on top, cover the pan with a lid and allow the dish to simmer for 5 minutes over high heat.

*Stay true to your style; this brings
tranquility and unity. You don't build
up a collection in a matter of days.
It comes with lifelong searching and
plenty of creativity.*

I'm especially alert when traveling, because that's when you can come across some unique finds. Those are what make all the difference. I walk into every large or small interior design store. I rummage through garage sales and jumble sales and browse in small, unique boutiques. It is the mix of homemade, creative—sometimes expensive, but just as often cheap—items which makes my collection unique. It's all about creativity and it certainly doesn't have to cost a lot of money. Paint your table, pick flowers from the meadows, make your own cutting boards, sign up for a ceramics course... In short, let yourself be guided by your intuitive side.

This makes working in the kitchen so much more fun, and that's exactly where I find the most joy. All the items I use—whether it is the materials I work with, pots, bowls or plates—can be placed on the table. They make the dining experience more beautiful and fun—and I save on time because I have less washing up to do.

Would you like to enjoy a beautiful and convivial dining experience? Then think long-term. You don't have to stress when setting the table. Instead, from now on, keep your eye out for fun items and slowly but surely gather a collection of things that make you happy. Make sure to remain true to a particular style, because that gives clarity and peace and helps you make sure that everything goes well together. Start with the basics: a beautiful table. Are you not (or no longer) happy with it? Paint or sand your table or leave it outside in the wind and rain for a year. That's what I recently did with my own table. Is the table beyond saving and does it make you unhappy? Throw it out. Take a good look at your kitchen, decide what you do or don't like about it and get to work. Get your hands dirty and create your own world. You will be surprised at how much joy you will get out of it. And whatever you do—don't be afraid! An "imperfect" kitchen has so much more beauty and character than a picture-perfect kitchen.

ready in
15 minutes

carrots

with bacon and peas

- **3 large, fat carrots**
- **7 oz (200 g) diced bacon**
- **9 oz (250 g) strained tomatoes or tomato puree**
- **3½ oz (100 g) peas (fresh or frozen)**

Cook the diced bacon for approximately 4 minutes in a non-stick pan without any oil or fat. Meanwhile, slice the carrots into thin strands using a vegetable peeler. Add the strained tomatoes and the peas to the bacon, stir and then scatter the carrot strands on top. Cover the pan and allow to simmer for a few minutes until the carrots are just cooked. Stir everything carefully.

TIP: FRESH OR FROZEN PEAS
Fresh peas are the best, but you will only find these in the spring. Thankfully, frozen peas are a perfect alternative. They have the advantage that they've already been blanched, which means that you only have to heat them through at the end. Fresh peas should ideally be cooked about 4 minutes.

TIP: KETO
Replace the peas with relatively low-carb edamame beans (see cover).

This is probably the dish with the least work and the most flavor. It's so delicious.

*There's so much you can
do with eggplant.*

"Asian style" eggplant
and shrimp

- **1 lb (450 g) organic shrimp with tail (approx. 12 shrimp)**
- **2 eggplants**
- **¾ oz (20 g) ginger**
- **1½ oz (40 g) fresh cilantro**

Slice the eggplant into ¼-inch (½ cm) slices and then slice them again into sticks. Finely chop the ginger and add it to the eggplant sticks. Sauté the eggplant and ginger for 6 to 7 minutes until tender in some olive oil and season with salt and pepper. Stir occasionally. Push the vegetables to one side of the pan and cook the shrimp approximately 3 minutes in the same pan, next to the vegetables. Roughly chop the fresh cilantro and mix it in with the vegetables just before serving.

TIP: HERBS
Use plenty of ginger and cilantro, as they give this dish that typical Asian flavor. Are you not a fan of cilantro? Try using basil instead.

A juicy steak with velvety-smooth garlic and crunchy thyme—absolute bliss!

sirloin steak ✓ keto

with zucchini

- 10½ oz (300 g) sirloin steak
- 1 large zucchini (or 2 for big eaters)
- 1 head of garlic
- 1½ oz (40 g) fresh thyme (2 bunches, with soft stems)

– balsamic vinegar –

Slice the head of garlic in half horizontally across the middle (see the photo above). Slice the zucchini. Splash a bit of olive oil in a large frying pan, add the zucchini and place the two halves of the head of garlic in the pan with the cut side down. Do not turn the garlic over during cooking.
Sauté the vegetables over medium to high heat.

Season the meat with salt and pepper. After 7 minutes, push the vegetables over to one side and add the meat to the pan. Place the thyme sprigs alongside the meat. Add a little olive oil if necessary.
Cook the meat for 2 to 3 minutes on each side (or longer, depending on how you want your steak cooked).
Just before serving, drizzle a little balsamic vinegar over the zucchini.
Serve the meat with the zucchini, velvety-smooth garlic and crunchy thyme.

"new style" fried eggs ✓keto

with feta and mushrooms

- **4 eggs**
- **7 oz (200 g) feta or other cheese**
- **a little over 1 lb (500 g) mushrooms**
- **handful of chives**

Slice the mushrooms, cook them in olive oil and season with salt and pepper.

Separate the eggs into yolks and whites. Crumble the feta and mix it in with the egg whites.

Splash some olive oil into a pan and pour the feta mixture into the pan. Cook for approximately 5 minutes with the lid on. Meanwhile, finely chop the chives and mix together with the mushrooms.

As soon as the egg white has set and the feta is melted, spoon the mushrooms on top.

Make four wells in the mushroom heaps, place the egg yolks in the wells and serve.

*The deliciously cheesy bottom
makes all the difference.*

*A refined dish for when you need something
quick and special at the same time.*

fried fish ✓keto

with herbed vegetables

- **haddock fillet for 2 people**
- **3 oz (80 g) of your favorite olives**
- **4 tomatoes**
- **1 bunch fresh cilantro**

– butter –

Cook the fish over medium to high heat in plenty of butter. Turn the fish over just once if you can. Quarter the tomatoes. Remove the seeds over a sieve and collect the juice.

Dice the tomato. Press the leftover seeds down into the sieve to get all the remaining juice out. Chop the olives into pieces and finely chop the fresh cilantro. Add the diced tomatoes, olives and cilantro to the fish as soon as it is cooked. Add a little extra butter, if necessary. Cook for another 30 seconds and add the tomato juice. Season with salt and pepper. Place the fish on a dish or plate and spoon the vegetables with the delicious sauce over the top.

TIP: DICED TOMATOES
You should not cook the diced tomatoes. They should be warmed through at most.

This is undoubtedly bursting with flavor.

sautéed vegetables

✓ keto

with feta

- **1 large zucchini**
- **1 red pointed bell pepper**
- **7 oz (200 g) feta**
- **1½ oz (40 g) flat-leaf parsley**

Dice the zucchini into ½-inch (1 cm) cubes. Cook the diced zucchini in a generous splash of olive oil. Meanwhile, slice the bell pepper in rings. Cook them together with the zucchini for a total of approximately 12 minutes.

Dice the feta and coarsely chop the parsley. Add these to the vegetables and cook for an additional 2 minutes.

chickpeas

with tomatoes and onions

- **7 oz (250 g) cooked chickpeas**
- **2 tomatoes**
- **4 onions**
- **handful of fresh cilantro**

- ras-el-hanout -

Wash the chickpeas and place them in a pan with a splash of olive oil.
Scatter 2 tablespoons of ras-el-hanout over the chickpeas and cook for 3 minutes.
Scoop the chickpeas out of the pan.

Meanwhile, slice the tomatoes into thin slices and the onions into rings. Cook them in the same pan as the chickpeas in the leftover ras-el-hanout. After 5 minutes, return the chickpeas to the pan and heat everything through. Garnish the dish with some finely-chopped fresh cilantro just before serving.

TIP: LEFTOVER RECIPE
This is another one of my leftover recipes. Do you have leftover vegetables lying around? Cook them along with the tomatoes and onions! It will only make your dish that much tastier, and you get to clean out your fridge as well (also read p. 69).

Deliciously filling chickpeas for those days when you don't feel like meat or fish.

*So simple, so quick to make
—and so delicious!*

Chinese-style chicken ✓ keto

- **2 chicken breasts**
- **2 bunches spring onions (16 spring onions)**
- **2½ oz (70 g) unsalted roasted peanuts**
- **1½ oz (40 g) ginger**

– *2 garlic cloves* –

– *soy sauce* –

Remove the skins from the peanuts by rubbing them between your hands. You can easily remove the remaining skins by blowing on them. Let the peanuts soak for a while in a little bit of water. Chop the chicken into strips and cook them in olive oil or sesame oil.

Slice the ginger and spring onions into strips and add them to the chicken. Finely chop the garlic and add that as well. Add the drained peanuts and a splash of soy sauce to the dish and stir-fry until the chicken is cooked.

TIP: PEANUTS
Rub the peanuts between your hands to loosen the skins. Go outside and blow the skins away. If you are really strapped for time, you can leave the skin on or use pre-peeled peanuts.

mussels ✓ keto

in parsley sauce

- **3-4 lb (1½ kg) mussels**
- **1 bunch curly-leaf parsley (3½ oz/100 g)**
- **1 cup (250 ml) cream**
- **2 garlic cloves**

Rinse the mussels thoroughly. Finely chop the garlic and sauté in some olive oil in a large cooking pot. Finely chop the parsley. Add the cream and the chopped parsley to the garlic. Place the mussels in the cooking pot. Simmer covered over low heat for 5 to 7 minutes until all the mussels are open. Stir with a large spoon. Serve the mussels in a deep dish with the juices.

nori ✓keto

with crayfish and avocado

- 4½ oz (125 g) precooked crayfish
- 1 avocado
- 1 sheet nori seaweed
- 3 spring onions

– coarse salt –

Coat the nori sheet on one side with olive oil and scatter some coarse salt over the top. Roast the sheet for 3 minutes in an oven heated to 350 °F (180 °C) (see tip). Cut the avocado in half; remove the seed and scoop out the inside. Cut the avocado into small pieces and place in a bowl. Add the crayfish. Finely chop the spring onions and add them to the mixture.
Toss everything together and season with salt and pepper.
Place the nori sheet shiny side down on your worktop. Place the avocado mixture at the bottom of the sheet and roll it up firmly in the sheet. Slice the roll into two pieces and serve.

TIP: ROASTING NORI
You can skip this step, but roasted nori is crispier and tastier. If you do not roast the nori, it will soak up the moisture more quickly, making the nori tough and harder to bite into.

shrimp ✓keto

with tomato and basil

- **12 large, organic shrimp with tail (1 lb/400 g)**
- **3 tomatoes**
- **6 spring onions**
- **1 bunch of basil**

Finely chop the spring onions and separate the white and green parts. Add a generous splash of olive oil to a large frying pan. Place the white spring onion pieces in the middle and place the peeled shrimp around the center. Cook the shrimp and spring onions over medium heat. Quarter the tomatoes. Remove the seeds over a sieve and collect the juice. Turn the shrimp over.

Dice the pieces of tomato into cubes and place them with the spring onions in the center of the pan. Scatter the green spring onion pieces on top. Finely chop the basil and sprinkle over the shrimp. Drizzle the tomato juice over the shrimp as well. Season with salt and pepper and allow to simmer for another 30 seconds.

The sauce is particularly tasty and refined.

*For those days when
you don't feel like meat or fish
but still want something hearty.*

vegan portobello
✓keto

mushrooms

- **5 or 6 portobello mushrooms (1-1½ lb/500-600 g)**
- **handful of roasted peanuts**
- **10 spring onions**
- **4 garlic cloves**

– soy sauce –

Chop the portobello mushrooms into large pieces and cook them in sesame oil or olive oil. Finely chop the garlic and add the garlic to the mushrooms.

Slice the spring onions into 2-inch (5 cm) pieces. Slice the white part lengthways in two. Add them to the portobello mushrooms. Add the peanuts and a splash of soy sauce and serve.

salad ✓keto
with duck

- **3½ oz (100 g) dried or smoked duck breast, sliced**
- **1 carrot**
- **1 carton of garden cress**
- **handful of pine nuts**

– balsamic vinegar –

Roast the pine nuts for 6 minutes in an oven preheated to 350 °F (180 °C). Meanwhile, slice the carrots into thin strands using a serrated vegetable peeler. Add a splash of olive oil and some balsamic vinegar and season with salt and pepper. Add the pine nuts.

Toss the garden cress into the salad. Arrange the salad tastefully on a plate, place a few slices of duck breast on top and garnish with some extra balsamic vinegar.

A particularly surprising and refined salad.

When it needs to be fast, I want my food to be delicious, healthy and beautiful

Gone are the days when I would eat something quickly "to save time". Because I now realize that I have to pay for my five minutes of satisfaction with hours of feeling miserable, bloated and sleepy. I remember the day that it finally hit me. And from that day on, no more fast food for me. Meanwhile, for me it has become second nature to create quick, beautiful and healthy dishes. Quick doesn't have to mean boring, but it does mean that you have to be creative. Creating a quick, beautiful and healthy meal makes me happy for so many reasons: because it's quick and effortless; because I know I can eat a lot of it without feeling guilty or gaining weight; because this type of food leaves me with that blissfully satisfied feeling; because I know that I will still feel great the next day; because I know that this type of food nourishes my body instead of making me a slave to my cravings; simply because this food is the type of food that is delicious and makes me keep coming back for more.

My quickest go-to recipe, ready in 10 minutes
I also call this my **leftover recipe**, ideal for incorporating all those leftover vegetables:

vegetables + feta, halloumi, lentils or chickpeas + red or green curry paste

Step-by-step plan:
- Place all the vegetables on your countertop.
- First, chop vegetables such as root vegetables, carrots, fennel, green beans… into small pieces. These vegetables always need to cook longer.
- Cook them in a pot with a generous splash of olive oil and an equally large splash of water.
- Now, chop the softer vegetables such as tomatoes and onions into larger pieces and add them to the vegetables in the pan. Stir-fry until all the vegetables are cooked through.
- Stir in a couple of spoonfuls of curry paste.
- To finish, add diced feta, halloumi, lentils or chickpeas to the mixture. Stir-fry for another minute or two and remove from heat.
- Do you still have leftover fresh herbs such as flat-leaf parsley, cilantro or chives?
- Finely chop them and add them to the dish. Keep some aside to garnish.

Serving tips: how do you add flair to your stir-fry?
A stir-fry looks more appealing in a bowl or deep (pasta) dish. If you use a flat plate, use a cooking ring to give your dish some form. Garnish the dish with some fresh chopped herbs. Out of fresh herbs? In that case, use some dried thyme (this goes with practically anything); roasted sesame seeds; gomashio, a Japanese flavoring (see *The pantry* on p. 20) or seeds such as sunflower seeds. A fine example of this type of dish is the *Red vegetables with lentils* recipe on page 37.

sea spaghetti
with octopus

✓ keto

- **7 oz (200 g) cooked octopus tentacles**
- **4 oz (120 g) fresh or 1 oz (25 g) dried sea spaghetti (see tip)**
- **5 oz (150 g) strained tomatoes or tomato puree**
- **4 garlic cloves**

Rinse the fresh sea spaghetti under cold running water. Dried sea spaghetti needs to be soaked for 15 minutes in water first (or follow the directions on the packet). Finely chop the garlic and slice the octopus tentacles. Cook the garlic and tentacles in olive oil. After 3 to 4 minutes, add the drained sea spaghetti and cook for another couple of minutes. Add the strained tomatoes, season with salt and pepper and cook for another 2 minutes.

TIP: SEA SPAGHETTI
Sea spaghetti, also known as thongweed or buttonweed, is a type of algae. They're long, brown-green strands that look a lot like spaghetti. You can eat sea spaghetti both raw and cooked. It is rich in minerals and vitamins, making it incredibly nourishing. You can buy fresh and dried sea spaghetti in health food stores. The dried version is handy to have in your kitchen. It is really delicious and has a wonderful texture. You can also replace it with arame (sea oak) or hiziki (Japanese seaweed). Dried sea spaghetti increases five-fold in volume during the soaking process: 1 oz (25 g) dried sea spaghetti weighs approximately 4 oz (120 g) after soaking.

Once you have tried sea spaghetti,
you will definitely be making this again:
easy, really delicious and healthy.

ready in
20 minutes

veal medallions

with vegetables and mustard sauce

- **2 veal medallions**
- **10½ oz (300 g) brown mushrooms**
- **7 oz (200 g) spinach**

– soy sauce, mustard, butter –

Cook the veal medallions in the butter for approximately 5 minutes on both sides until browned. Meanwhile, slice the mushrooms. Wrap the medallions in aluminum foil and set aside. Pour off the fat, leaving any browned bits in the bottom of the pan. Melt another tablespoon or two of butter in the pan. Cook the mushrooms until all the moisture has evaporated. Add 3 tablespoons mustard, 3 tablespoons water and 3 tablespoons mild soy sauce. Stir until you have a smooth sauce. Push the mushrooms off to one side of the pan and place the spinach next to it. Cover the pan and allow the spinach to wilt.

Add the meat back to the pan. Also add the juices that have seeped out of the meat. Warm through thoroughly and serve.

A delicious classic.

Filled with wonderfully full flavors
guaranteed to make everyone happy.

curry

with chicken and red bell peppers

- **2 chicken breasts**
- **2 red bell peppers**
- **1 glass coconut milk (approx. 10 tablespoons)**
- **3 tablespoons mild red curry paste**

– dried thyme –

Slice the chicken into strips and cook them in olive oil. Meanwhile, slice the bell pepper into strips (see tip) and add them to the chicken. Simmer gently over medium heat for approximately 10 minutes until the bell pepper has softened. Stir occasionally to make sure the bell pepper doesn't burn, otherwise your sauce will turn gray.

Pour in the coconut milk. Add a tablespoon of curry paste to the dish and taste. You can add a second spoonful if you want for more flavor. 2 or 3 tablespoons are usually enough. Stir well and allow everything to cook through. Serve in a deep plate or dish and garnish with some dried thyme.

TIP: SLICING BELL PEPPERS
Cut the stem away from the bell pepper. Place the bell pepper upside down on a cutting board. Cut the sides from the bell pepper from the top down. That way you won't have any trouble with the seeds, and you will have nice straight pieces to slice into strips or cubes.

Deliciously creamy mozzarella always tastes good.

casserole ✓keto

with delicious Italian flavors

- **1 to 2 balls fresh mozzarella cheese**
- **10½ oz (300 g) spinach**
- **4 tomatoes**
- **2 tablespoons capers**

– Herbes de Provence or oregano –

Preheat the oven to 350 °F (180 °C). Take an ovenproof pan. Slice the tomatoes and remove the hard, white core. Season with some salt, pepper and Herbes de Provence. Cook the tomatoes for approximately 6 minutes in a generous splash of olive oil. Cover the pan to allow the tomatoes to cook quicker. Stir occasionally. Add the spinach to the tomatoes and let the spinach wilt for approximately 3 minutes. Tear the mozzarella into pieces and divide it over the vegetables. Sprinkle the capers and some Herbes de Provence over the top. Place the pan in the oven for 5 minutes.

TIP: AMOUNTS
Are you feeling hungry? Use two balls of fresh mozzarella. I often find that one ball of mozzarella with plenty of vegetables is enough for two people.

You can serve these crunchy crackers with almost anything.

nut and seed crackers ✓ keto

Ingredients for a 20 by 30 cm sheet:
- **3½ oz (100 g) roasted hazelnuts or mixed nuts**
- **3½ oz (100 g) flaxseeds or mixed seeds**
- **2 beaten eggs**
- **2 sprigs rosemary**

Preheat the oven to 350 °F (180 °C). Mix the nuts and the seeds in a blender. Remove the leaves from the rosemary sprigs and add them to the nuts and seeds. Blend into a coarse flour.

Mix in the eggs. Line a baking dish with parchment paper. Spread a layer of the nut and seed mixture over the bottom. Place a second sheet of parchment paper on the mixture and rub evenly over the paper using a tea towel until the dough is no more than ¼ inch (½ cm) thick. Remove the top sheet of parchment paper. Place the dish in the oven. Turn the cracker over after 10 minutes and cook for an additional 5 minutes.

TIP: AMOUNTS
Use 1 egg per 3½ oz (100 g) of mixed nuts and seeds.
Use your favorite nuts and seeds: pumpkin seeds, sesame seeds, flaxseeds, pecans, walnuts, pistachios …

quinces
with dry-cured ham and hazelnuts

- **2 quinces**
- **15 slices or 5 oz (150 g) dry-cured ham, very thinly sliced**
- **2 oz (50 g) roasted hazelnuts**

– butter –

Rinse the quinces and remove the fuzzy skin on the outside. Remove the core and slice the quinces into semicircles. Cook them over medium heat in a generous tablespoon or two of butter. After a couple of minutes, add a generous amount of water to quicken the cooking process. They cook more easily that way. Turn the quince pieces over after 4 minutes and cook them another 3 minutes until soft and light brown. Keep an eye on them; quinces tend to burn easily. Coarsely chop the nuts. Place the quinces in a rose pattern. Tear the ham into pieces and place them between the quince slices. Season with black pepper and garnish with the nuts and a slight drizzle of olive oil.

TIP: QUINCE

Never call a quince a pear. A quince is more like an apple with a pear shape. I am not such a big fan of pears, but I love quinces. They have everything I love: the right texture, not too hard or too soft; and the perfect taste, not too sweet and with a hint of sour. I find quinces both beautiful and mysterious. If you pour some water in a pan full of quinces while they're being cooked, a jelly-like substance immediately appears. That's why quinces were traditionally used to make quince jelly. But I don't do jellies. Quince tastes so much better when you just cook it, and it's ideal to use in a salad or even in a fruity breakfast. You should always cook quinces, because they're hard and inedible when raw. You should also cook quinces longer than you would normal pears. Make sure they don't burn because they cook very quickly especially towards the end.

*Once you've tried quince, you'll want more.
This is such a divine dish.*

steak ✓ keto

with vegetables

- **large steak for 2 people (9-10½ oz or 250-300 g)**
- **7 oz (200 g) broccolini**
- **1 red pointed bell pepper**
- **¾ oz (20 g) ginger**

– *soy sauce* –
– *cider vinegar* –
– *olive oil or butter* –

Preheat the oven to 325 °F (160 °C). Slice the bell pepper into thin rings and the ginger into very thin matchsticks. Cook the steak for approximately 3 minutes in olive oil or butter until browned and then place the pan in the oven for 4 to 5 minutes. Adjust the cooking times according to the thickness of the steak and the desired texture. Cook the ginger and bell pepper in olive oil. Halve the broccolini lengthways and add to the bell pepper. Add a splash of water and stir-fry until the broccolini is cooked al dente. Add a splash of soy sauce and cider vinegar to the vegetables.

Remove the meat from the oven, let it rest for a few minutes, and then slice into thin slices. Place the meat on a plate and arrange the vegetables alongside it. Place the ginger on the meat and spoon the sauce over the top.

stir-fried chicken ✓ keto

with vegetables and peanuts

- **2 chicken breasts**
- **2 carrots**
- **1 leek**
- **handful of unsalted peanuts**

– soy sauce –

Slice the chicken into very thin strips and mix with olive oil. Stir-fry the chicken for three minutes.
Slice the leek into 4-inch (10 cm) strips and add them to the chicken. Stir-fry for approximately
5 minutes until the chicken and leeks are cooked. Add 3 tablespoons soy sauce and season with
black pepper.
Slice the carrots into thin strands using a vegetable peeler and stir-fry them together with
the chicken and leeks for two minutes.
Coarsely chop the peanuts. Spoon the chicken and vegetables onto a plate and garnish with
the chopped peanuts.

This dish makes everyone happy, both young and old.

large shrimp
with ras-el-hanout and vegetables

✓ keto

- **10½ oz (300 g) organic shrimp with tail (frozen)**
- **4 large tomatoes**
- **7 oz (200 g) spinach**
- **½ cup (100 ml) cream**

- ras-el-hanout -

Hold the frozen shrimp under running water and pull them apart. The shrimp can still be frozen, but they should no longer stick together. Heat a pan with a dash of olive oil. Cook the (still frozen) shrimp for about 2 minutes. Sprinkle them with 2 small teaspoons of ras-el-hanout and cook for another two minutes.

Meanwhile, slice the tomatoes. Remove the shrimp from the pan, even though they may not be quite cooked through, and place them on a plate. Put the tomato slices in the pan with the leftover juices; this gives the tomatoes a delicious flavor. Put a lid on the pan and allow to simmer for 6 to 8 minutes. Stir the tomatoes and place the spinach on top. Add the cream, cover the pan again and allow to simmer for an additional 3 minutes. Stir the vegetables and season with salt and pepper to taste.

Place the shrimp on top of the vegetables and cook a little longer to combine all the flavors and the yellow color of the ras-el-hanout. Serve in an attractive serving dish.

chicken keto

with vegetables and cashew sauce

- **2 chicken breasts**
- **2 red bell peppers**
- **7 oz (200 g) broccolini**
- **3½ oz (100 g) cashews**

Chop the bell peppers into pieces (see tip: Curry with chicken and red bell peppers on page 89) and cook them with a splash of olive oil. Stir regularly to make sure that the bell pepper doesn't burn, otherwise your sauce will turn gray. Slice the chicken into thin strips and add them to the bell peppers. Remove the hard stalks from the broccolini and add the soft parts to the pan. Add half of the nuts. Season generously with pepper and allow to cook a few minutes longer.

Place the remaining nuts in a blender and add approximately 1 cup (200-300 ml) of water. Blend to a thick milk-like consistency. There will still be some small nut pieces, but that's fine. Pour the cashew nut milk into the dish. Allow to simmer until the sauce thickens. Serve in deep dishes.

Once you have made this wonderful dish a couple of times, you'll be able to make it in less than 15 minutes.
Then you can savor it to the fullest!

Liver is probably the
healthiest meat around,
but you either love it or hate it.

chicken livers

with apples

- **7 oz (200 g) chicken livers**
- **2 red apples**
- **1 pomegranate**

– soy sauce, butter or olive oil –

Cleaning chicken livers is easy. Trim away any white or green bits and anything else that may look unsavory. Slice the pomegranate in half. Squeeze the juice out from one half, as if you're squeezing an orange. Remove the seeds from the other half (see tip). Dice the apple and cook in some butter or olive oil. After 6 minutes, add the chicken livers and cook them for 1 minute on each side. Add 4 tablespoons of soy sauce and the pomegranate juice. Season with black pepper. Cook for a few more minutes to allow the sauce to thicken. Stir the pomegranate seeds in just before serving.

TIP: LIVER
We used to eat a lot of organ meat; today, it's mostly muscle.
However, organs are still the most nutritious meats.
Predators will always go for the organs first when eating
their prey. We may have forgotten about it, but liver
really is very tasty.

TIP: POMEGRANATE
Hold the pomegranate cut-side down over a bowl and tap the skin with a solid object.
I use the grip of a knife sharpening steel, for example. This way, you can tap the seeds
out of the fruit. You need to scoop out the last of the seeds by hand. Remove the white
skins that come out with the seeds.

pizza ✓keto

- 3½ oz (100 g) ground almonds
- 2 eggs
- 3½ oz (100 g) grated gruyere cheese
- 7 oz (200 g) strained tomatoes or tomato puree

– dried Herbes de Provence –

Preheat the oven to 350 °F (180 °C). Mix half the gruyere with the ground almonds and the eggs. Knead it into a dough and split into two balls. Place them on a sheet of parchment paper. Place a second sheet of parchment paper on top and flatten using a tea towel to make a "crust" that is about ¼ inch (½ cm) thick. Remove the top sheet of parchment paper. If the edges of the pizza crust have cracked a little, press them slightly towards the middle. Bake the bases in the oven for 7 minutes until the dough is light brown in color and cooked through. Add a splash of olive oil to the strained tomatoes and season with black pepper, a little bit of salt and a generous sprinkling of Herbes de Provence.

Spread the sauce out over the pizza bases and divide the remaining cheese over the top of each pizza. Sprinkle with some extra Herbes de Provence and cook the pizzas another 3 minutes in the oven until the cheese has melted.

You can serve me this simple pizza any time. Delicious!

quinoa risotto

- **5 oz (150 g) uncooked quinoa**
- **2 to 3 tablespoons mascarpone**
- **9 oz (250 g) brown mushrooms**
- **8 spring onions**

Slice the mushrooms and sauté them for 2 minutes in some olive oil. Finely chop the white part of the spring onions. Add them to the mushrooms and cook for another minute. Meanwhile, rinse the quinoa and add to the mushrooms. Mix everything together. Add twice as much water as quinoa. Season with salt and pepper and cook for 12 minutes until the water has evaporated and the quinoa is soft. The best way to find out whether it's done is to taste it. If the quinoa is still too hard, add a little bit of water and cook a little longer.

Stir the mascarpone into the quinoa risotto and season with salt and pepper. Spoon the risotto onto a plate. You may want to use a cooking ring. Garnish with the green part of the spring onions, sliced diagonally into thin rings.

A creamy, surprising dish.

creamy cauliflower
with feta and mushrooms

- **1 small head of cauliflower**
- **7 oz (200 g) feta**
- **9 oz (250 g) brown mushrooms**
- **¾ oz (20 g) chives**

Thinly slice the outer tips of the cauliflower florets to produce small crumbs.
Chop the rest of the cauliflower into large pieces. Cook the pieces in water until tender.
Finely chop the mushrooms. Cook the onions in olive oil and add the cauliflower crumbs
after a couple of minutes. Drain the cooked cauliflower and remove from the heat. Crumble
the feta into the cauliflower and mash it all into a creamy puree.

Finely chop the chives and mix together with the mushrooms. Spoon some cauliflower
puree on a plate and place the fried mushrooms and cauliflower crumbs on top.

A surprising dish with an unusual combination of flavors.

spinach ✓keto
with spicy ricotta and egg

- **14 oz (400 g) spinach**
- **7 oz (200 g) ricotta**
- **3 eggs**
- **3 tablespoons red curry paste**

Preheat the oven to 400 °F (200 °C). Sauté the spinach in an ovenproof cooking pot. Mix the ricotta together with the red curry paste. Carefully fold the ricotta mixture into the cooked spinach. Beat the eggs and briefly mix them into the spinach, making sure that not all of the spinach is covered with egg. Cook on the stovetop for 2 minutes and then place the pan in the oven for 5 minutes.

TIP: CURRY PASTE
Add the curry paste one spoonful at a time and taste between spoonfuls to make sure that your ricotta doesn't get too spicy.

A spinach omelet bursting with flavor.
Also ideal for when you're on the go.

Things can get pretty swinging in the kitchen,
especially on a beautiful sunny day.
I throw open all the doors and walk in and out
of the kitchen, barefoot as always. Blackened
feet are part of it all, and a thorough scrubbing
in the evening does wonders. And the next day?
I just start all over again.

ready in
25 minutes

A dish bursting with sunshine, color and delicious flavors.

oven-baked
salmon ✓keto
with vegetables

- **1 large fennel bulb**
- **2 to 3 tomatoes**
- **1 large onion**
- **salmon fillet for 2 people**

– dried thyme –

Preheat the oven to 350 °F (180 °C). Line a large baking dish with aluminum foil. Coat the foil with olive oil. Slice the fennel into ¼-inch (½ cm) thick slices and thinly slice the tomatoes and onions. Place them on the baking dish. Drizzle the vegetables with some olive oil and season with salt, pepper and some dried thyme. Place the tray in the oven and bake for 20 minutes.

Scatter some dried thyme over the salmon, season with salt and pepper and drizzle some olive oil on top. Cook the fish with the vegetables in the oven during the final 10 minutes of cooking. Place the salmon on a plate and spoon the vegetables over and next to the salmon.

hearty
chickpea soup

- **9 oz (250 g) cooked chickpeas**
- **2 leeks**
- **1 large onion**
- **2 to 3 tablespoons green curry paste**

- ras-el-hanout -

Slice the onions and sauté them in a pan with a splash of olive oil until they are golden brown. Transfer them, together with the oil, to a plate and set aside. Slice the leek into rings and sauté for a couple of minutes in olive oil. Make sure that the rings don't turn brown. Add two cups of water and stir in a tablespoon of ras-el-hanout. Add the curry paste one tablespoon at a time and taste the soup to make sure it doesn't get too spicy. Allow the soup to simmer for 5 minutes or until the leeks are cooked through. Add the chickpeas and cook for a few more minutes. Divide the soup over the plates. Garnish with the fried onion rings. Don't forget to add the olive oil from the onion rings; it tastes delicious. Spoon a bit of it over the soup to create some gorgeous pearls of flavorful oil.

duck breast
with a cranberry crust

- 1 duck breast
- 3½ oz (100 g) dried cranberries (unsweetened)
- 1 lb (500 g) bok choy (2 to 3 large stalks)
- 2 oz (50 g) pine nuts

– soy sauce –

Preheat the oven to 350 °F (180 °C). Soak the cranberries in water. Trim most of the fat from the duck breast. Drain the cranberries and grind them together with the pine nuts and a teaspoonful of olive oil. Season with salt and pepper. Coat the duck breast with the paste and put the meat in a baking dish. Bake in the oven for 12 to 15 minutes.

Roughly slice the bok choy and sauté in some olive oil. Add a splash of soy sauce once it is tender and season with black pepper.

Remove the duck breast from the oven and allow it to rest. Slice the meat into thick slices. Do so carefully so the cranberry crust doesn't fall off.
Serve with the cooked bok choy.

This dish always makes my husband happy.

Shrimp are always a success.
The ever so slightly sour hint from the
cider vinegar combines wonderfully
with the sweetness of the carrots.

large shrimp ✓keto
with vegetables

- **1 lb (450 g) large frozen shrimp (approx. 12 shrimp)**
- **1 bunch of green asparagus**
- **2 carrots**
- **fresh cilantro**

- *2 garlic cloves* -
- *cider vinegar* -

Peel the shrimp. Slice the garlic. Cook the shrimp together with the garlic in some olive oil.
Turn them over after 2 minutes and cook them for another minute. Add a generous splash of cider vinegar. Season with salt and pepper and cook for a little bit longer. Remove the shrimp from the pan.

Slice the green asparagus into 4-inch (10 cm) pieces and cook them in the leftover shrimp juices.
If necessary, add a little more olive oil and cider vinegar.

Slice the carrots into thin strands using a vegetable peeler and stir-fry them with the asparagus for about 2 minutes. Add the shrimp and heat through. Season with salt and pepper.
Garnish the dish with some finely chopped fresh cilantro just before serving.

It's amazing what delicious flavor combinations you can create with so few ingredients.

ground chicken
with tomato sauce, onion and flaked almonds

keto

- 10½ to 14 oz (300 to 400 g) ground chicken
- 2 large onions
- 5 tomatoes
- ¾ oz (20 g) flaked almonds

- ras-el-hanout -

Preheat the oven to 350 °F (180 °C). Mix 2 tablespoons of ras-el-hanout into the ground chicken and shape the meat into two fat sausages. Place the chicken sausages in a baking dish and bake them for about 15 minutes in the oven. Slice the onions into wafer-thin slices and fry them until browned in some olive oil. Spoon them out of the pan and transfer them to a plate. Thinly slice the tomatoes and add them to the same pan with an extra splash of olive oil and a small glass of water. Cook for about 5 minutes, stirring regularly, until you have a thick sauce. Season with salt and pepper.

Remove the chicken sausages from the oven. Spoon the tomato sauce over the chicken, place the onions on top and garnish with the flaked almonds. Return to the oven until the almonds are brown and crunchy.

quinoa
with stir-fried vegetables

- 1 large glass of quinoa (approx. 5 oz (150 g), uncooked)
- 1 raw red beet (9 oz/250 g)
- 9 oz (250 g) brown mushrooms
- 3 red onions

– soy sauce –

Rinse the quinoa under cold running water. Put the quinoa in a cooking pot and add twice the amount of water. Bring to a boil. Meanwhile, peel the red beet under running water (see tip). Dice it into ½-inch (1 cm) cubes and add these to the quinoa. Add a generous splash of olive oil and season with plenty of black pepper and a little bit of salt. Cover the pot and let simmer for about 12 minutes. Slice the onions in rings and the mushrooms in slices. Sauté them in plenty of olive oil until soft. Once they're cooked, season with salt and pepper and add a generous splash of soy sauce.

Check the quinoa regularly to make sure it doesn't burn. Use a cooking ring to serve your quinoa and spoon the vegetables over the quinoa.

TIP: PEELING RED BEETS
Want to avoid getting red fingers after peeling beets? Peel them under running water.

brown shrimp ✓keto

with cauliflower

- 1 small head of cauliflower
- 7 oz (200 g) small, precooked brown shrimp
- 1 oz (30 g) flaked almonds
- handful of flat-leaf parsley

– butter –

Clean the cauliflower. Do not remove the stem or the outer leaves (see image). Slice 2 thick ½-inch (1 cm) slices from the center of the cauliflower. Roast the flaked almonds with some butter in a pan until they are golden brown and season with salt and pepper. Remove them from the pan and set aside. Cook the cauliflower slices in a covered pan with butter and a generous amount of water. Turn them over only once, after about 6 minutes. The total cooking time is about 12 minutes. Mix the precooked shrimp with the finely chopped flat-leaf parsley and some olive oil. Season with salt and pepper. Place the cauliflower on a plate, spoon the shrimp on top and garnish with some flaked almonds.

This is a heavenly dish. Pure flavors that are sure to appeal to everyone.

quinoa tortillas

- **4 eggs**
- **5 oz (150 g) quinoa (uncooked)**
- **5 oz (150 g) + ¾ oz (20 g) (for garnish) spinach**
- **1 large onion**

Finely chop the onion and sauté for a couple of minutes in olive oil. Add the quinoa and stir. Add twice the volume of the quinoa in water (see tip) and allow to cook for 12 minutes, or until the quinoa is cooked through and the water has evaporated. Add a little extra water if the quinoa is not fully cooked. In a separate pan, sauté the spinach in a splash of olive oil. Drain, making sure to remove all the moisture (see tip), and add to the quinoa. Allow everything to cool a bit before you add the eggs, otherwise the eggs will set as soon as you add them. Mix the eggs into the quinoa-spinach mixture. Spoon some of the mixture into a pan and flatten it out. Cook for about a minute and turn the tortilla over. Cook another minute on the other side. Once you get the hang of it, you can cook 2 to 3 tortillas at a time. Serve the tortillas with some freshly chopped spinach.

TIP: COOKING QUINOA
Add two parts of water per part of quinoa. I put the quinoa in a glass to measure it out. I add two glasses of water per glass of quinoa.

TIP: SPINACH
I cook the spinach in a separate pan because spinach loses a lot of moisture during the cooking process, causing your 'batter' to become watery. Make sure to press as much moisture out of the spinach as possible before adding it to the quinoa.

*This is a really fun dish to make.
Everyone loves this and it's also
ideal for on the go.*

Definitely give this a try.
You won't know what hit you!

carrots
with an Asian touch

- **2 carrots**
- **2 organic blood oranges**
- **2 oz (60 g) roasted hazelnuts**
- **handful of pitted black olives**

– butter –

Preheat the oven to 400 °F (200 °C). Wash the oranges thoroughly and slice them thinly. Line a baking sheet with aluminum foil, coat the foil with olive oil and place the oranges on the tray. Drizzle with some olive oil and bake in the oven for 20 minutes. Slice the carrots into diagonal pieces and sauté them for about 5 to 7 minutes in plenty of butter. Coarsely chop the nuts. Arrange the orange slices on a plate, add the carrots and top with the olives and nuts. Season with some black pepper and a little bit of salt.

TIP: BLOOD ORANGES
Blood orange slices baked in the oven taste heavenly. I sometimes serve them as chips. You need to cook them just long enough for the skin to turn crunchy without letting them burn. That's when they're at their best. In my oven, that's after exactly 20 minutes at 400 °F (200 °C). But each oven is different, so you'll have to experiment with it the first time.

Ode to the tomato

Yes, I use a lot of tomatoes, because I think they're delicious, unique and healthy. The tomato adds color and flavor to a dish like no other vegetable and provides a natural sauciness to boot. The tomato originates from the New World and the name stems from the Aztec word "tumatl". By way of the Italian kitchen, the "pomodoro" or golden (oro) apple (pomo) finally made its way up to us in Northern Europe. Today, the tomato is one of the most harvested vegetables worldwide. You will find them in all sorts of colors, shapes and flavors and they are a true joy to work with in the kitchen.

It may surprise you to find that I'm not really a fan of raw tomatoes. But, you can serve me cooked tomatoes any time. I usually only eat raw tomatoes when they're in season, because an average supermarket tomato can't even begin to compare to a high-quality, ripe tomato. That's why I'm convinced that people who claim not to like tomatoes are probably eating the wrong tomatoes and not ripe tomatoes of the finest quality. Moreover, tomatoes and fats go together: a slice of tomato with olive oil, some black pepper and fleur de sel tastes amazing. The fat enhances the flavor, the quality, and the health benefits of the tomato (see below). I find cooked tomatoes irresistible, but here too, I always choose quality tomatoes. Sauté them with plenty of olive oil and season them with a generous amount of freshly ground black pepper and a little bit of salt; that's when the power of the tomato really shines through.

Tomatoes and health

Tomatoes are part of the nightshade family and that puts many people off. Nightshade vegetables are believed to cause a build-up of acids in the body and to be the cause of all sorts of health conditions. But, the toxic substances characteristic of the nightshade family are only found in unripe tomatoes. In ripe tomatoes, these substances have been converted and are therefore no longer dangerous.

As with most vegetables (although botanically speaking, the tomato is technically a fruit), tomatoes are refined, leaving behind very few toxic substances; and even then, those are only found in unripe fruits. What's more: recent studies have shown that these substances are linked to positive health benefits. We still don't fully realize how healthy the tomato really is, on all fronts. Tomatoes have potential antibiotic and anti-carcinogenic properties (especially in the prevention of prostate cancer), they are a preventive food for cardiovascular diseases (tomatine binds with cholesterol, reducing cholesterol uptake in the body), and they also counter fluid retention in the body. These features are enhanced when the tomatoes are cooked together with olive oil or mashed to a pulp. That's when the cell walls are destroyed, releasing substances such as lycopene. This means that cooked tomatoes are not only tastier (or at least, I think so…), they are also much healthier and therefore a must-have in every kitchen.

For the science behind this text, I was inspired by the work of Dr. Sc. Pharm. Paul Nijs. I had the honor of previewing his book *Laat voeding uw medicijn zijn* (Let food be your medicine). This book, a standard reference of all edible fruit and vegetable types, will probably be published in 2019 and is a basic reference book for doctors, dieticians, experts and anyone who is interested in knowing more about the relationship between food and health.

Let the oven do the work

salmon ✓keto
with asparagus, tomato and olives

Preparation time: 5 minutes - Cooking time: 20 minutes

- **2 salmon fillets**
- **1 bunch of green asparagus**
- **3 tomatoes**
- **3½ oz (100 g) of your favorite olives**

– balsamic vinegar –
– dried thyme –

Preheat the oven to 350 °F (180 °C). Dice the tomatoes, halve the olives and slice the asparagus diagonally into 2-inch (5 cm) pieces. Put the vegetables in a baking dish and season with salt and pepper. Pour in a generous amount of olive oil and balsamic vinegar and toss everything carefully together. Push the vegetables off to the sides of the dish and put the salmon in the middle. Completely cover the salmon with dried thyme and season with some salt and pepper. Drizzle the olive oil over the salmon in a thin stream until the thyme is completely covered with oil. Place the dish in the oven and bake for about 20 minutes.

A baked dish that's guaranteed to please everyone, including the cook.

spicy baked cauliflower
with halloumi

✓ keto

Preparation time: 8 minutes - Cooking time: 30 minutes

- **1 cauliflower (approx. 1 lb/500 g)**
- **7 oz (200 g) halloumi**
- **3½ oz (100 g) pumpkin seeds**
- **3 or 4 garlic cloves**

- ras-el-hanout -

Boil some water in a pan and preheat the oven to 350 °F (180 °C). Slice the cauliflower into large florets and cook them for about 5 minutes in the boiling water. Drain and pour a generous amount of olive oil over the cauliflower. Season with 2 tablespoons of ras-el-hanout. Stir thoroughly but carefully until the cauliflower florets are completely covered with the yellow spice mix.

Spoon the cauliflower into a baking dish and bake in the oven for 20 minutes. Do not rinse the cooking pot just yet.
Finely chop the garlic and dice the halloumi. Take the cooking pot with the leftover fat and ras-el-hanout and cook the garlic and pumpkin seeds for about 2 minutes. Add the halloumi. Spoon the cheese mixture over the cauliflower and serve.

This is without a doubt one of my favorite dishes.
Truly bursting with flavor.

Is healthy eating liberating or limiting?

Lots of people still have the wrong idea about "eating healthy". They immediately think of restrictions and are afraid that they will not have enough willpower. But why do we think that? I suppose it has to do with the traditional approach to healthy eating, which is all about reducing your calorie intake: eat less, eat only low-fat, avoid fats, count your calories, starve yourself… which makes everyone unhappy, including me. And the worst of it is —it doesn't work.

Look around you. Half the population is overweight, and we can say with confidence that the traditional approach has failed. This has nothing to do with willpower, which is what we so frequently hear, but it does have to do with the wrong advice. There is no way that you can keep up with the dietary advice that we used to get, which was all about restrictions, and that's what creates the dreaded yoyo-effect.

Thanks to scientific progress, we now know better. I invite you to discover the latest insights on nutrition with an open mind. People who take that first step, and are open to it, immediately realize that being successful at eating healthier has little to do with willpower. Many people who eat according to the recommendations made in this book experience it as liberating. It takes some time for some people to find what works for them and for their bodies to adjust, but after a while people notice that they can eat lots of tasty food, that they always feel satisfied after a meal and, most of all, that their diet is healthier and more varied. This has little to do with willpower, and everything to do with respecting your own body. And that's what it's all about. We shouldn't be struggling with our bodies but working together with them. That is the liberation that people experience, and it feels like coming home. We shouldn't be forcing our bodies by sheer willpower but rather nourishing them with good food; you will see and feel that your body will do what it needs to do. It is so simple: nourish your body with high-quality, full, natural ingredients and let your body do the rest. You will be surprised at how easy it is.

zucchini pie ✓ keto

Preparation time: 12 minutes - Cooking time: 20 minutes

- **2 zucchini (green, yellow or mixed)**
- **3 eggs**
- **handful of flat-leaf parsley**
- **7 oz (200 g) gruyere cheese**

Preheat the oven to 350 °F (180 °C). Mix the eggs together with the parsley and three quarters of the gruyere. Thinly slice the zucchini. The easiest way to do this is to use a mandolin. Line a round baking dish or springform pan with parchment paper and pour half of the mixture into the dish. Arrange the zucchini slices on top in a circular pattern (see photo).
Pour the rest of the egg mixture over the zucchini and sprinkle the remaining gruyere on top. Bake in the oven for 20 minutes.

Ideal for brunch or lunch.

dry-cooked salmon
with oven-baked vegetables

Preparation time: 12 minutes - Cooking time: 30 minutes

- **salmon fillets for 2 people, without skin**
- **approx. 15 cherry tomatoes**
- **8 spring onions**
- **14 oz (400 g) pumpkin or winter squash**

- dried thyme -
- balsamic vinegar -
- soy sauce -

Preheat the oven to 350 °F (180 °C). Divide the salmon fillet into 4 pieces. In a small bowl, pour in a splash of balsamic vinegar and add one large teaspoon of dried thyme, plenty of pepper and a little bit of salt. Marinate the salmon fillets in the marinade while preparing the vegetables.

Peel the squash and dice into ½-inch (1 cm) cubes. Put them in a baking dish. Remove the outer stalks from the spring onions, slice them in half and then in half again. Put them together with the tomatoes in the dish. Season with salt and pepper and pour a generous amount of olive oil and some soy sauce over the vegetables. Toss everything carefully together and place the salmon fillets among the vegetables. Put the baking dish in the oven and bake for 30 minutes.

TIP: PUMPKIN OR WINTER SQUASH
Make sure you dice the pumpkin or winter squash into small enough pieces, otherwise they won't cook in 30 minutes.

This is undoubtedly one of my favorite dishes.
All the ingredients that I love, simply cooked in the oven.

Beefsteak tomatoes are a joy to look at and make perfect tomatoes for stuffing.

stuffed ✓keto
tomatoes
with feta and zucchini

Preparation time: 10 minutes - Cooking time: 20 minutes

- **2 beefsteak tomatoes or other large tomatoes**
- **1 zucchini**
- **7 oz (200 g) feta**
- **1 bunch of chives**

Preheat the oven to 350 °F (180 °C). Finely grate the zucchini. Line a bowl with a clean tea towel and spoon the grated zucchini into the bowl. Mix in some salt. Meanwhile, finely chop the chives and hollow out the tomatoes. Squeeze as much of the moisture as you can out from the zucchini by twisting the tea towel. Pour off the liquid and put the zucchini back in the bowl without the towel. Mix a generous amount of olive oil into the zucchini mixture. Season with salt and pepper and mix in the chives. Crumble the feta into the zucchini and mix thoroughly. Place the hollowed-out tomatoes in a baking dish and fill them with the zucchini mixture. It doesn't matter if some of it spills over the side. Bake the stuffed tomatoes for 20 minutes in the oven.

*Deliciously soft vegetables
with crunchy chickpeas.*

oven-baked chickpeas
with vegetables

Preparation time: 6 minutes - Cooking time: 25 minutes

- **1 can cooked chickpeas (approx. 12 oz/350 g when drained)**
- **1 eggplant**
- **2 onions**
- **10½ oz (300 g) cherry tomatoes**

– ras-el-hanout –

Preheat the oven to 350 °F (180 °C). In a bowl, put the drained chickpeas and add a generous splash of olive oil. Mix in one generous tablespoonful of ras-el-hanout, mix well and leave it aside to rest. Dice the eggplant into 1-inch (2 cm) cubes. Coarsely chop the onions and slice the cherry tomatoes in half. Line a baking dish with aluminum foil, and place the eggplant, onions and tomatoes on the foil. Drizzle some olive oil over the vegetables, season with salt and pepper and mix thoroughly. Make sure that the diced eggplant is completely covered in olive oil. Scatter the chickpeas on top and bake for 25 minutes in the oven until the vegetables are tender.

This kind of baked dish creates pure happiness.

chicken ✓keto
with zucchini, yogurt and red curry

Preparation time: 10 minutes - Cooking time: 35 minutes

- **4 chicken drumsticks**
- **5 oz (150 g) full-fat or Greek yogurt**
- **2 zucchini**
- **3 tablespoons red curry paste**

– *olive oil or butter* –

Preheat the oven to 350 °F (180 °C). Cook the chicken drumsticks for a couple of minutes in olive oil or butter until golden brown on the outside. Meanwhile, slice the zucchini into matchsticks and add to the chicken. Cook together with the chicken for a few seconds (see tip: Fat). Mix the curry paste together with the yogurt and pour into a baking dish. Spoon the chicken and the zucchini into the dish. Cover the drumsticks with the yogurt mixture and coat the vegetables with it as well but leave some of the zucchini uncovered. Put the baking dish in the oven for 25 minutes.

TIP: FAT
Pour the cooking fat off if it gets too dark or burnt when cooking the chicken. Add some fresh butter or oil before adding the zucchini to the chicken.

TIP: YOGURT
Definitely use full-fat or Greek yogurt. This reduces the chance of the yogurt separating. If that does happen, that's fine. It doesn't change the taste of this dish.

chicken
with vegetables and honey

Preparation time: 10 minutes - Cooking time: 30 minutes

- **2 chicken breasts**
- **1¼ lb (600 g) pumpkin or winter squash**
- **¾ oz (20 g) sesame seeds**
- **liquid honey**

– soy sauce –

Preheat the oven to 350 °F (180 °C). Slice the chicken and the winter squash into strips measuring ½ by 1½ inches (1 by 3 cm).

Scoop the chicken and squash into a baking dish and add the sesame seeds. Mix 4 tablespoons honey with 4 tablespoons soy sauce and 2 tablespoons olive oil to make a thick sauce. Stir the sauce into the chicken and winter squash and bake for about 30 minutes in the oven, or until the chicken and squash are both tender and the sauce has become syrupy. Regularly stir the chicken and vegetables to prevent them from charring.

TIP: OVEN TIMES

This dish is completely cooked through in 30 minutes in my oven but remember that each oven is different. Stir the chicken and vegetables regularly and keep an eye on them, especially towards the end of the cooking process. The sauce needs to be syrupy, but it can burn easily towards the end of the cooking time.

Gorgeous chicken with delicious caramelized vegetables.

chicken ✓keto

with carrots and tomatoes

Preparation time: 12 minutes - Cooking time: 1 hour

- **2 chicken thighs**
- **4 plum tomatoes**
- **3 carrots**
- **lime**

- ras-el-hanout -
- soy sauce -

Preheat the oven to 350 °F (180 °C). Place the chicken thighs in a baking dish (you can halve them if you wish, as I have done). Season with a tablespoon of ras-el-hanout and pour a generous amount of olive oil over the top. Rub the chicken with the oil and spice mixture.

Slice the carrots into thin strips using a vegetable peeler.
Put the carrot strips in a bowl. Dice the tomatoes and remove the hard, white core.
Add the diced tomato to the carrots. Add the juice of half a lime and pour a splash of soy sauce and olive oil over the vegetables. Season with salt and pepper and knead the carrots and the tomatoes until the carrots turn soft.

Place the vegetables around the chicken and pour the juices in as well. Cover the baking dish with aluminum foil. Make a hole about ½ inch (1 cm) in diameter in the foil to allow the moisture to escape. Bake in the oven for 1 hour. Remove the foil after 50 minutes and return to the oven for the final 10 minutes.

TIP: PLUM TOMATOES
I like to use plum tomatoes in baked dishes because they do not contain as much moisture. Do you still have too much moisture left in your dish after baking? Pour it off and serve the liquid as a broth or starter. Don't throw it away, it's incredibly delicious!

This deliciously spicy chicken combines wonderfully with velvety, tender vegetables.

rack of lamb ✓ keto

with tomatoes and seaweed

Preparation time: 10 minutes - Cooking time: 20 minutes

- **1 rack of lamb**
- **3 tomatoes**
- **4 oz (120 g) fresh or 1 oz (25 g) dried sea spaghetti**
- **a few sprigs of rosemary**

- garlic -

Dice the tomatoes, remove the hard, white core and cook the tomatoes for about 7 minutes in a generous splash of olive oil until you have a thick sauce. Rinse the fresh sea spaghetti thoroughly and add to the tomatoes. If you use dried sea spaghetti, you will have to soak it in water for 15 minutes first. Season with salt and pepper and allow it to simmer a little longer. Preheat the oven to 350 °F (180 °C). Cook the rack of lamb for 3 minutes on each side in olive oil. Generously season the meat with pepper and a bit of salt and add a couple of crushed garlic cloves. Remove the rosemary leaves from the stems. Add them to the meat and bake everything for 6 minutes in the oven.

Slice the rack of lamb between the bones into pieces. Place them on a plate and spoon the thick tomato sauce with the sea spaghetti next to it. Garnish with the crunchy cooked herbs.

*A dish with lamb always
brings happiness to the table.*

lamb ✓keto
with vegetables and candied lemons

Preparation time: 8 minutes - Cooking time: 1 hour and 10 minutes

- **1 lb (400-500 g) leg of lamb (see tip)**
- **5 tomatoes**
- **7 oz (200 g) spinach**
- **1 candied lemon**

Preheat the oven to 350 °F (180 °C). Cut the meat into large pieces and brown them, stirring constantly, in olive oil in an ovenproof pan. Slice the tomatoes and add them to the meat. Season with salt and pepper. Pour in a small glass of water. Cover the pan and allow it to cook for 1 hour in the oven. Slice the candied lemon into quarters, remove the pulp and slice the peel into strips (the pulp of candied lemons is not used).

Take the pan out of the oven and stir the meat and tomatoes to create a thick stew. Add the lemon peel and the spinach. Let the spinach wilt and serve.

TIP: LEG OF LAMB

A leg of lamb is much too big for two people. That's why I sometimes replace it with pieces cut from the leg of lamb. This is easier than cooking a large leg of lamb. You can also use lamb stew meat for this dish.

lamb ⊘keto

with vegetables

Preparation time: 10 minutes - Cooking time: 1 hour and 40 minutes

- **2 slices from a leg of lamb**
- **5 tomatoes (1 lb/500 g)**
- **4 oz (120 g) black olives**
- **2 onions**

- dried rosemary -

Preheat the oven to 350 °F (180 °C). Brown the slices from the leg of lamb in a pan with some olive oil and season with plenty of pepper and a little salt. Dice the onions and the tomatoes and put them in a baking dish. Add the olives and a generous splash of olive oil. Season with salt, pepper and dried rosemary. Toss everything together. Add the meat to the baking dish and cover with aluminum foil. Bake in the oven for an hour and a half.

Lamb is tasty, easy to prepare and makes the kitchen smell so inviting.

Delicious! The delicate flavor of the mozzarella is enhanced by the warm vegetables.

mozzarella
with warm vegetables

Preparation time: 7 minutes - Cooking time: 20 minutes

- **8 medium-sized tomatoes**
- **2 balls mozzarella cheese**
- **2½ oz (40 g) basil**
- **1 zucchini**

- dried thyme -

Preheat the oven to 350 °F (180 °C). Slice the tomatoes into quarters and slice three quarters of the zucchini into ½-inch (1 cm) slices. Slice the zucchini slices in half. Spoon the vegetables into a baking dish, drizzle with a generous splash of olive oil and season with dried thyme, salt and pepper. Toss everything together well. Bake in the oven for 20 minutes. Mix the remaining zucchini with the basil and a generous amount of olive oil in the blender to make a pesto. Season with salt and pepper. Spoon the vegetables onto a plate.

Tear the mozzarella into pieces and place them with the vegetables. Spoon some pesto over the top and garnish with a drizzle of olive oil.

parsnips
with feta and nuts

Preparation time: 8 minutes - Cooking time: 45 minutes

- **2 parsnips (10½-14 oz or 300-400 g)**
- **7 oz (200 g) feta**
- **¾ oz (20 g) parsley**
- **2 oz (60 g) hazelnuts**

Preheat the oven to 350 °F (180 °C). Slice the parsnips into thin strips. To do so, first slice them lengthwise in half, then in half again, and then once more.

Coat the strips with olive oil and place them in a baking dish.

Bake in the oven for 40 minutes.

Finely chop the parsley and coarsely chop the hazelnuts. Crumble the feta. Mix in a generous splash of olive oil and season with a bit of salt and a generous amount of freshly ground black pepper.

Divide the mixture over the parsnips and return to the oven for another 5 minutes.

A scrumptious vegetarian dish. Not only exceptionally delicious, but also a pleasure to look at.

chic

*An exquisite dish
to start off your menu.*

salmon ✓keto

with herb sauce

Preparation time: 4 minutes - Cooking time: 6 minutes

- **5 oz (150 g) salmon fillet without skin**
- **1 oz (30 g) sundried tomatoes**
- **½ bunch chives**
- **handful of pine nuts**

– balsamic vinegar –

Preheat the oven to 400 °F (200 °C). Put the salmon in a baking dish and season with salt and pepper. Put the pine nuts next to the fish and bake in the oven for 6 minutes. Finely chop the sundried tomatoes and the chives. Add a splash of olive oil and the balsamic vinegar and season with salt and pepper.

Remove the salmon from the oven and coarsely chop the pine nuts. Mix them in with the tomatoes. Place a piece of salmon on a plate and spoon the sauce over the top.

TIP: HERB SAUCE
You can combine this delicious sauce with anything. Keep this recipe on hand, because it can make all the difference with a simple piece of meat, fish or even cheese.

A particularly festive and flavorful dish.

canard à l'orange
(duck with orange sauce)

Preparation time: 12 minutes - Cooking time: 20 minutes

- **1 duck breast, with skin**
- **5 tangerines (or 3 oranges)**
- **5 sprigs fresh rosemary**
- **handful of pistachios**

Score the duck breast skin down to the meat every ¼ inch (½ cm) with a sharp knife. Put an ovenproof non-stick pan over high heat and cook the duck breast, skin side down and without any oil or butter. Cook the fillet for 3 minutes, turn it over and cook the other side for an additional 2 minutes. Meanwhile, peel 4 of the tangerines (or 2 of the oranges). Remove the segments and halve them down the middle. Pour out the fat from the pan and drizzle a generous amount of olive oil into the pan. Add the tangerines to the meat in the pan. Squeeze the juice from the remaining tangerine (or orange) over the meat. Season with a generous amount of freshly ground pepper. Put the pan in the oven for 10 to 15 minutes at 350 °F (180 °C).

Meanwhile, remove the rosemary leaves from the stems and finely chop them. Chop the pistachios (or put them in a blender). Add some olive oil to the rosemary and the nuts and season with salt and pepper. Sprinkle the nut mixture over the duck 7 minutes before the end of cooking, so that the nuts and herbs become nice and crunchy without burning them. Slice the duck breast fillet, pour some of the sauce over the duck and serve straight from the pan.

salmon ceviche ✓keto

Preparation time: 6 minutes - Cooking time: none

- **14 oz (400 g) salmon fillet, without skin**
- **2 limes**
- **¾ oz (20 g) fresh cilantro**
- **1 red onion**

Slice the salmon into large pieces and season with salt and pepper. Slice the onion into wafer-thin rings and finely chop the fresh cilantro. Mix the onion with the fresh cilantro, the juice from the limes and a generous splash of olive oil. Spoon the salmon into the marinade and allow to soak for 2 minutes. Serve.

TIP: CEVICHE
When I was in Peru, I had the most delicious ceviche, one of the most popular local dishes. Ceviche is raw fish marinated in citrus juices. Onions, chili peppers and garlic are usually added, and the dish is generously seasoned with salt and pepper. Make sure that the fish is ultra-fresh, because you're eating it raw. The fish is usually marinated in the sour marinade for a while, giving you the impression that the fish is lightly cooked. I learned in Peru that ceviche tastes best when it's served immediately.

pan-fried octopus ✓keto
with leeks

Preparation time: 7 minutes - Cooking time: 15 minutes

- **7 oz (200 g) cooked octopus tentacles**
- **2 leeks**
- **roasted sesame seeds**

– butter, coconut oil or sesame oil –
– balsamic vinegar –
– soy sauce –

Wash the leeks and slice them into thin strips. Fry a handful of the white part of the leek in a pan with butter, coconut oil or sesame oil, until the leek is light brown and crunchy. Remove from the pan and drain on a paper towel. Sauté the remaining leek in plenty of olive oil or sesame oil and season with salt and pepper. Stir regularly to prevent the leek from burning. Slice the octopus into rings. Take a second pan and cook the octopus rings in olive oil. After 2 minutes, add a generous splash of balsamic vinegar and soy sauce. Keep cooking until the sauce becomes syrupy. Divide the cooked leek over the plates, place some of the octopus around the leek and garnish with the crunchy leek whites and the sesame seeds.

TIP: COOKED OCTOPUS TENTACLES
Although these are commonly called "tentacles", the octopus, a member of the cephalopod family, actually has eight "arms". Cephalopod arms have suckers for the entire length while tentacles just have them at the ends. Octopus meat tastes similar to that of the white squid, but it has a subtler flavor and texture.
You can sometimes buy raw octopus at the market, although they usually have it frozen rather than fresh. You can also find cooked octopus in the supermarket nowadays. It's ideal to have around the house, because it's a quick way to make a salad or an exquisite dish.

If you want to surprise someone with a deliciously sensual dish, then I would certainly recommend this.

The crunchy flat-leaf parsley
makes all the difference.

smoked salmon ✓ keto
with crunchy flat-leaf parsley

Preparation time: 6 minutes - Cooking time: 3 minutes

- **5 oz (140 g) smoked salmon**
- **3½ oz (100 g) flat-leaf parsley**
- **2 spring onions**
- **1 jar of salmon roe**

Preheat the oven to 350 °F (180 °C). Keep a quarter of the parsley aside. Remove the leaves from the remaining parsley, put them in a bowl, and pour a little bit of oil over them. Season with some salt and toss everything together. Scatter the parsley over a baking dish and bake for 3 minutes in the oven. Finely chop the spring onions and the remaining parsley and put it all in a bowl. Mix in a splash of olive oil and cider vinegar. Season with some salt and pepper. Place a piece of salmon on a plate (see tip) and spoon the herbed spring onions over the top. Place a second piece of salmon on top of the first. Top it off with the crunchy flat-leaf parsley and garnish with some scattered salmon roe.

TIP: CHIC SALMON CIRCLES
You can just place the salmon pieces on top of each other, but if you want to make them into nice circles, use a cooking ring. Don't worry if the salmon slices aren't big enough. Place the salmon slices on a cutting board so they overlap each other and use the cooking ring to cut out circles. Then use a spatula to transfer the circular slice of salmon to a plate. If you are short on time, or don't feel like the extra work, simply place the salmon slices on top of each other without cutting them.

raw salmon ✓ keto

with nori tapenade

Preparation time: 8 minutes - Cooking time: none

- **salmon (1½ oz/40 g per person for a snack and 3 oz/80 g for a starter)**
- **4 sheets nori seaweed**
- **¾ oz (20 g) pine nuts**
- **roasted sesame seeds**

- cider vinegar -
- fleur de sel -

Tear the nori sheets into pieces and blend them together with a generous splash of olive oil and cider vinegar along with the pine nuts to make a tapenade. Season with some salt and pepper. If needed, add a little extra olive oil and cider vinegar. Slice the salmon, place it on a plate and spoon the tapenade over the top. Scatter some fleur de sel over the dish just before serving.

TIP: TAPENADE
This tapenade is delicious with practically any fish dish, but it also goes really well on a cracker (see page 93).

191

The crunchy skin combines wonderfully with the velvety-soft, tender salmon and the sweet spring onions.

pink-cooked salmon ✓keto
with crunchy skin and sautéed spring onions

Preparation time: 8 minutes - Cooking time: 12 minutes

- **2 pieces of salmon, with skin**
- **10½ oz (300 g) spring onions**
- **1 glass white wine**

- cider vinegar -
- soy sauce -
- butter -

Preheat the oven to 350 °F (180 °C). Using a broad, sharp knife, slice the skin away from the salmon. Take a piece of parchment paper and place the salmon skins on one side. Coat them with olive oil and season with pepper and just a hint of salt. Fold the parchment paper over the skins and weigh them down with something heavy, like a baking dish. Bake in the oven for about 10 minutes. Put half the olive oil and half the butter in a pan and put the pan over medium-high heat. Cook the salmon in the oil and butter. Slice up the white part of the spring onions and add them to the salmon. After 3 minutes, turn the fish over and lower the heat. Add the wine, a splash of cider vinegar and a splash of soy sauce to the salmon. Let the sauce reduce for about 4 minutes. Finely chop the green part of the spring onions and add half to the salmon. Allow to cook for a little longer. You will use the other half of the spring onions to garnish the dish. Place the salmon on a plate, spoon the spring onion sauce over the salmon and top it off with the crunchy salmon skin. Garnish with the freshly chopped spring onions.

TIP: CRUNCHY SALMON SKIN
The salmon skin almost looks like a chip and creates a wonderful combination with the tender salmon. You can slice the skin in pieces beforehand or break them into pieces afterwards.

sea bass ✓ keto

with vegetables

Preparation time: 5 minutes - Cooking time: 10 minutes

- **2 sea bass fillets, with skin**
- **3 tomatoes**
- **3 tablespoons capers**
- **¾ oz (20 g) basil**

– soy sauce –

Cook the fish skin-side down in a large pan with olive oil.
Quarter the tomatoes. Remove the seeds over a sieve and collect the juice. In the sieve, press out the remaining moisture from the seeds and the pulp. Dice the quartered tomatoes. Finely chop the basil.

Turn the fish over. Add the capers, diced tomatoes, basil, tomato juice and a generous splash of soy sauce. Cook for another minute. Serve the fish on a plate and spoon the vegetables and the sauce on top.

*Conjure up a gorgeous
dish with refined flavors
and have it on the table
in no time.*

quick desserts

sautéed strawberries

with ricotta and honey

Preparation time: 4 minutes - Cooking time: 5 minutes

- **approx. 10 strawberries**
- **7 oz (200 g) ricotta**
- **5 sprigs rosemary**
- **2 to 3 tablespoons honey, to taste**

Remove the leaves from the rosemary sprigs. Add some olive oil to a pan and cook the leaves from 1 sprig for a minute until they are nice and crunchy. Remove them from the pan and drain on a paper towel.

Quarter the strawberries, pour some extra oil in the pan and sauté the strawberries for about 2 minutes with the remaining rosemary leaves. Mix the ricotta with 1 or 2 tablespoons of honey, depending on your taste, and divide over 2 glasses. Spoon the strawberries with the sauce over the ricotta mixture and garnish with the crunchy rosemary leaves.

A fantastically scrumptious dessert in less than 10 minutes.

oven-baked apples

Preparation time: 8 minutes - Cooking time: 25 minutes

- **2 apples**
- **7 oz (200g) ricotta**
- **3 to 4 tablespoons honey**
- **handful of flaked almonds**

- 1½ oz (40 g) butter -

Preheat the oven to 350 °F (180 °C). Spread the ricotta over the bottom of a baking dish. Melt the butter and add 3 to 4 tablespoons honey. Slice the apple into ½-inch (1 cm) slices, remove the core and place the apple slices on top of the ricotta.
Spoon some of the honey-butter mixture over the apple, scatter some flaked almonds on top and drizzle with the remaining sweetened butter.
Bake in the oven for 25 minutes. If you want to serve this as a dessert, one or two apple slices per person should be enough.

*This tastes so good, but it's more than just a dessert;
we sometimes eat it for Sunday lunch.*

creamy chocolate cake

Preparation time: 6 minutes - Cooking time: 15 minutes

- 1½ oz (40g) coconut flour
- 4½ oz (120 g) chocolate (>75% cocoa)
- 3½ oz (100 g) thick coconut milk (see tip)
- 2 eggs

– coconut sugar to taste –
(or other sugar)
– extra: parchment paper –

Set a little bit of the chocolate aside for the garnish. Melt the rest of the chocolate (see tip on page 206). Mix the eggs together with the coconut flour and the coconut milk. Add the sugar and the melted chocolate. Make sure that the chocolate is not too hot, otherwise the eggs will set! Line a small baking dish with parchment paper and pour the mixture into the dish. Bake the dish for 15 minutes in a preheated oven at 350 °F (180 °C). Garnish with some finely chopped chocolate.

This chocolate cake is at its best when it's still warm, but it does make it harder to cut. This cake is also delicious served cold!

TIP: COCONUT MILK
Ideally, use coconut milk with a creamy consistency. If your coconut milk is watery, use less of it.

frozen chocolate pralines

Preparation time: 15 minutes - Cooking time: 20 minutes

Ingredients for about 20 pralines:
- **1 banana (approx. 3½ oz/100 g)**
- **3½ oz (100 g) peanut butter**
- **3½ oz (100 g) chocolate**
- **2 oz (50 g) ricotta**

Mash the bananas and then mix in the peanut butter and the ricotta. Make small heaps on parchment paper using two teaspoons. Put in the freezer for 20 minutes until they have hardened.
Melt the chocolate (see tip) and dip the cooled heaps into the chocolate. Put the pralines on parchment paper. The chocolate will immediately set because of the frozen filling. Serve immediately or store in the freezer until you're ready to serve.

TIP: MELTING CHOCOLATE
You can melt chocolate in a *bain marie*, but I put the chocolate in a stainless-steel bowl and put it for a few minutes in an oven at 140 °F (60 °C). The chocolate will continue to melt as you take the bowl out of the oven. I find it to be a quick and easy way to melt chocolate. Please note: don't ever let chocolate cook, because then you will have to start all over again.

Chic pralines to impress the one you love.

delicious dessert

with mascarpone and blueberries

Preparation time: 4 minutes - Cooking time: 15 minutes

- **7 oz (200 g) mascarpone**
- **5 oz (150 g) blueberries**
- **2 eggs**

– 1 oz (30 g) coconut sugar –

Preheat the oven to 350 °F (180 °C). Separate the eggs into yolks and whites. We only need the yolks. You can save the whites for another recipe, if you wish.
Mix the egg yolks and the sugar with the mascarpone and stir in the blueberries. Spoon into ramekins or small ovenproof bowls and place them in the oven for 13-15 minutes.

This must be the easiest and tastiest dessert ever.

ricotta-chocolate cake

Preparation time: 8 minutes - Cooking time: 25 minutes

Ingredients for 4 people
(or for 2 people if you want large slices ☺)
- **2 eggs**
- **9 oz (250 g) ricotta**
- **1 oz (25 g) coconut flour**
- **5 oz (150 g) chocolate callets (85% cocoa)**

– 1 oz (30 g) coconut sugar –
(or other sugar)

Preheat the oven to 350 °F (180 °C). Beat the eggs with the sugar for 3 minutes. Add the ricotta and the coconut flour and mix. Stir the chocolate callets into the batter. Put the mixture into a cake tin. Bake the cake in the oven for 25 minutes. Allow the cake to cool before cutting it.

TIP: LUKEWARM CAKE
This cake tastes best when it's still lukewarm, but it'll still be soft, making it harder to cut. The cake will set as it cools.

TIP: HOW MUCH SUGAR?
The less sugar and sweeteners you eat, the less you'll crave sugar. Moreover, things quickly tend to become too sweet. 1 ounce (30 grams) of coconut sugar is more than enough for me, but feel free to add more sugar for a sweeter cake.

TIP: CHOCOLATE CALLETS
Chocolate callets are small chocolate discs or pearls (like chocolate chips) to be used in desserts. Can't find them? In that case, use regular chocolate and chop it into fine pieces.

Need to make an irresistible cake in no time? No problem!

*The combination of warm chocolate
and molten peanut butter is heavenly.*

warm, soft chocolate
with peanut butter

Preparation time: 7 minutes - Cooking time: 13 minutes

Ingredients for 2 large servings (or 4 small servings)
- **2 eggs**
- **1 oz (30 g) butter**
- **3½ oz (100 g) chocolate (85% cocoa)**
- **peanut butter (see tip)**

– 1 oz (30 g) sugar –
(or none, to taste)

Melt the butter with the chocolate in the oven at 175 °F (80 °C). Beat the eggs with the sugar to make a thick, fluffy mixture. Stir the melted chocolate carefully through the eggs. Spoon a couple of teaspoons of the chocolate mixture in a ramekin or small bowl and put a tablespoon of peanut butter in the middle. Spoon some more of the chocolate mixture on top and bake for 13 minutes in an oven at 175 °F (80 °C) (see tip).

TIP: PEANUT BUTTER

These are many varieties of this product, which is really just roasted peanuts ground into a paste. I do not even like to use the word peanut butter, because it is not really "butter". However, you can easily make peanut butter yourself. Just blend the peanuts for 5 to 10 minutes in a food processer until you have a creamy paste.

TIP: 175 °F

That's right: 175 °F and not 375 °F. This allows the egg to set while making sure that the chocolate stays nice and creamy. This tastes so good. The big advantage is that you can use beautiful bowls, which normally can't be used in the oven. Put the bowls containing the chocolate in a cold oven and heat them up gently. Fine ceramics break with sudden temperature changes.

Flower petals

Everyone at our house knows the rule: withered
flowers are not to be thrown away. Flowers that are
starting to wilt have a special beauty to me; their colors
become more intense, and their drooping petals give
them a touch of melancholy. They complement my life
and add narrative to my home.

When the petals are somewhat dry but haven't started
to rot just yet, I pluck the petals from the buds and
lay them out to dry on a sunny windowsill. I then
scatter the intensely colored dried leaves over the
table during my next dining experience. Then, I put
on some wonderful evocative music, which I have
compiled onto my CDs *Puur Genieten 1 & 2* and I whip up
something delicious. And that's how my flowers start
their second life.

2CD

PASCALE NAESSENS

puurgenieten2

muziek voor
sfeervolle
tafelmomenten

Pascale's other major passion
besides writing is designing.
She is a ceramic artist and her
ceramics are sold worldwide.
Over the last few years, she has
been focusing more on designing.
Her central focus is the dining
table and everything that comes
with it. She has designed glasses,
utensils, earthenware, pots and
pans, tables and chairs, and she
compiles CDs.

"My happiness lies in creating,
in making my small world
more beautiful and intense.
That's what I want to share with
the world. I hope to inspire
people to do the same."

ingredient index

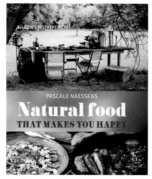

ISBN: 978 94 014 1983 3

ISBN: 978 1 4197 2617 0

www.lannoo.com
www.purepascale.com

Would you like further information?
Contact publisher: Uitgeverij Lannoo, gunther.spriet@lannoo.be, www.lannoo.com
Contact author: Pascale Naessens, info@purepascale.com, www.purepascale.com

RECIPES, TEXTS, STYLING AND CONCEPT: Pascale Naessens
PHOTOGRAPHY: Roos Mestdagh, Wout Hendrickx and Ramon de Llano
DESIGN AND LAYOUT: Kris Torfs - Gemex Publishing bvba
ENGLISH TRANSLATION: Textcase, Deventer

The ideas and recipes in this book serve as a source of inspiration and as part of a varied menu for healthy people. Anyone suffering from a condition should consult a doctor or health professional at all times. The information in the book should not be used as medication or as a substitute for any form of medical treatment.

If you have any comments or questions, please do not hesitate to contact the editor:
redactielifestyle@lannoo.com

© Pascale Naessens and Uitgeverij Lannoo nv, Tielt, Belgium, 2019
D/2019/45/344 – NUR 440-441
ISBN: 978 94 014 6148 1